TH.
THE EUMENIDES

NOTES

including
- *Introduction and Backgrounds*
- *Life of Aeschylus*
- *Summaries and Commentaries*
- *Character Sketches*
- *Suggested Reading*
- *Examination Questions*

by
Robert J. Milch
Brooklyn College

INCORPORATED

LINCOLN, NEBRASKA 68501

Editor

Gary Carey, M.A.
University of Colorado

Consulting Editor

James L. Roberts, Ph.D.
Department of English
University of Nebraska

Cliffs Notes, Inc.   Lincoln, Nebraska

CONTENTS

INTRODUCTION

Tragedy and drama as we know them in the western world were born with Aeschylus, one of the greatest dramatists and poets of all time. Aeschylus lived and wrote more than 2,000 years ago in the city of Athens in Greece, during one of the most extraordinary periods in European history. In values, background, and circumstances he was completely a man of his century, and yet, perhaps because of this, his works have a special inner harmony and vitality, a confident outlook, and a grasp of the quality of human life, that give them meaning in all times and places. *The Oresteia* is a product of Aeschylus' maturity. It is his last known work and a worthy monument to the genius for which he is renowned.

The tragic drama of Aeschylus arose in a world very different from ours, although contemporary western civilization has its roots in that world. The commentaries and background material in this book will enable you to understand these differences so that you can appreciate the plays of Aeschylus more fully. When you understand what is different about them and why, you will also be able to see clearly those things that have not changed in these three tragedies—the eternal questions that are still pondered by thoughtful men, the keen insights into the nature of God, justice, and human life.

But remember—a summary is not a substitute for the complete work, and the ideas in a commentary are only intended to help you to evaluate the plays and develop your own ideas about them. If you neglect to read these plays in full or to give them the attention to which they are entitled, you fool no one and cheat only yourself.

BACKGROUND OF GREEK TRAGEDY

Tragedy was performed in Athens at the three annual festivals of Dionysus, the most important of which was the Great, or City, Dionysia in late March. On three successive mornings at this festival, three tragic poets, who had been selected competitively earlier in the year, each presented a tetralogy consisting of three tragedies and a satyr-play. In addition, the festival featured comic and dithyrambic contests, and religious processions and rituals of various kinds. At the close of the festival ten judges who had been chosen by lot determined the winners and awarded prizes.

Besides writing the plays and composing the accompanying music, the poet was responsible for directing the production and supervising rehearsals. Often, in earlier times, he acted the role of the *protagonist,* or central character, also, but this tradition seems to have been broken in the time of Sophocles. The poets chosen to compete at the festivals were assigned actors, chorus, extras, and musicians by the state. The costs of the production were paid by the *choregus,* a wealthy citizen appointed by the government to do this as a *liturgy,* or public service. The privilege of backing the plays was considered a great honor, and the *choregus* shared the praise and awards given the poet if their plays won first prize.

Because attendance was a civic and religious obligation as well as a source of entertainment, admission to the theater was originally free. When it eventually became necessary to charge for tickets, the state provided funds for all citizens who could not afford the price.

ORIGINS

Tragedy is thought to have developed from the ancient dithyramb, or choral lyric, which was sung by a male chorus in honor of the god Dionysus at his annual festivals. These performances also included group dancing and probably some brief dialogue between the leader and the chorus. At first the dithyramb was a crude improvisation based on the myths about Dionysus and may have taken the form of a rough burlesque or satire, from which the satyr-play of classical drama was derived. In time it came to have a more formal artistic structure and its content was expanded to include stories from the whole legendary tradition.

At some point a radical transformation in approach took place and a serious philosophical attitude replaced the older boisterousness. The addition of an actor to the chorus allowed more complicated and lengthy stories to be used. The father of drama was said by the Greeks to have been Thespis. He first used an actor in his productions and was responsible for several other innovations. In 534 B.C. Thespis put on the first tragedy at the festival of Dionysus in Athens, although his new dramatic form may have been in existence for a short while before this in the rural areas of Attica.

There is some reason to believe, however, that it was Aeschylus who first wrote tragedy in the sense that the word is used today, with emphasis on content rather than stylistic matters. During the fifth century tragedy matured and its technique was improved until it became the sophisticated literary form seen in the hands of Sophocles.

Regardless of the changes in style and content, tragic performances remained an important element in the civic worship of Dionysus. The dithyramb also developed along independent lines as a choral medium, and dithyrambic contests continued to be a regular part of the dramatic festivals at Athens along with tragedy for the next few centuries.

PLOTS

The stories used in tragedy were taken almost exclusively from the great cycles of mythology, although occasionally, as in *The Persians* of Aeschylus, a poet might draw upon a contemporary theme. These ancient myths and heroic legends were like a bible to the Greeks, for they recorded what was thought to be the collective social, political, and religious history of the people, and included many profound and searching tales about the problems of human life and the nature of the gods. The custom requiring the use of these mythological stories in tragedy satisfied an essential requirement of the religious function of drama, for it enabled the poets to deal with subjects of great moral dignity and emotional significance.

From a dramatic point of view, the use of plots and characters already familiar to the audience gave the poet many opportunities for the use of irony and subtle allusions that are not available to the modern playwright. Suspense as it is known in the present-day theater could not easily be evoked, but the audience's attention was held by the poet's freedom to change or interpret the myths as he thought necessary. The spectators, already aware of the outlines of the story, learned from tragedy what personal motives and outside forces had driven the characters to act as they did. It is thought that the dramatist's reinterpretation and explanation of the ancient myths was one of the most important factors considered by the Greeks in evaluating his work.

The solemn and exalted quality of Greek tragedy, and the purposeful examination of the meaning of life in which its characters engage, are even today able to make a deep impression on readers, and are direct results of the use of stories based on mythological themes.

THE THEATER AND THEATRICAL EQUIPMENT

The Greek theater was built in the open air and was generally quite large; the Theater of Dionysus at Athens, for example, had more than 17,000 seats. The theaters were usually built in hollowed-out hillsides, and despite their size had excellent acoustics, so that words spoken by the performers could easily be heard in all sections.

The *theatron* was the area in which the audience sat. It was shaped like a horseshoe and had rows of stone seats rising upward and backward in tiers. In the first row were stone thrones for the principal citizens and the priest of Dionysus.

The circular area at ground level which was enclosed on three sides by the U-shaped *theatron* was known as the *orchestra,* or dancing place of the chorus. In its center was the *thymele,* an altar to Dionysus on which sacrifices were made and which was sometimes used as a stage prop during plays. The chorus assembled in the *orchestra* after marching in through the right or left *parodos*, or entrance passage, and remained there during the rest of the performance. The flute player and occasional harpist who provided musical accompaniment for the tragedies generally sat in a corner of the *orchestra*.

On the side of the *orchestra* which formed the open end of the *theatron* stood a wooden structure, the *skene*, or scene building. This was a dressing room for the actors, but its facade was usually made to resemble a palace or temple and it served as a backdrop for the action of the play. The three doors of the *skene* were used for entrances and exits.

The *proscenium* was the level area in front of the *skene* on which most of the play's action took place, although at times the actors might move to the *orchestra* or even to the roof of the *skene*. There was no stage, but the *proscenium* may have been raised one step higher than the *orchestra*, and there was no curtain.

A few items of technical equipment were available for special effects. These included devices for imitating lightning and the sound of thunder; other noisemakers; painted scenery; the *eccyclema*, a wheeled platform which was rolled out of the *skene* to reveal a tableau of action that had taken place indoors (e.g., at the end of *Agamemnon* where the doors of the palace are opened to show the bodies of the dead king and Cassandra, also at the end of *The Choephori*); and the "machine," some kind of derrick that could be mounted on the roof of the *skene* and used to bring about the miraculous appearances of gods.

The actors performed in elaborate formal costumes and wore masks that emphasized the dominant traits of the characters they were impersonating. All members of the cast were male. They had to be competent singers as well as actors because many of their lyrical lines were chanted to music. The mode of acting seems to have been conventional and stylized rather than naturalistic, but it could not have been too artificial, since many scenes call for lively, realistic action.

On the whole, tragic performances must have been very stately and colorful spectacles, in which a pageant-like quality was derived from the brilliant costumes and organized movements of large numbers of players and extras, and the blending of drama, poetry, music, and dance to create a solemn yet entertaining act of devotion to the gods.

THE CHORUS

The chorus was the nucleus from which tragedy evolved and it continued to have a central place in the drama throughout classical times. The use of the chorus varied, depending on the method of the playwright and the needs of the play being performed, but most often it acted as the "ideal spectator," as in *King Oedipus,* wherein it clarifies the experiences and feelings of the characters in everyday terms and expresses the conventional attitude toward developments in the story.

In some plays, like *The Suppliants* of Aeschylus, the chorus was itself a central figure in the tragedy rather than a group of interested bystanders, and this had a direct effect on the size and nature of its role, but usually the chorus was not so closely involved in the action of the drama. In general the tragedians used the chorus to create a psychological and emotional background to the action through its odes, to introduce and question new characters, to point out the significance of events as they occurred, to establish facts and affirm the outlook of society, to cover the passage of time between events, and to separate *episodes.*

The trend in tragedy was toward a decline in the importance of the chorus, caused mainly by the introduction of additional actors and increasing sophistication in their dramatic use, and by the more personal and complex nature of the stories selected for dramatization. With the passage of time the proportion of choral to individual lines decreased significantly, and the dramatic functions of the chorus, aside from the continued use of choral odes between *episodes,* were greatly reduced.

At a typical performance of tragedy in the fifth century, the chorus marched into the *orchestra* chanting the *parodos* and remained drawn up there until the end of the play. At various points it divided into semi-choruses and moved around in the *orchestra* to suit the requirements of the play, but its most important moments came when it chanted the choral odes to music, accompanied by stylized gestures and a series of intricate group dances. At times the chorus also engaged in a lyrical dialogue, or *kommos,* with one of the characters and made brief comments or inquiries during the course of an *episode.*

STRUCTURE

Classical tragedies were composed within a definite structural framework, although there are occasional minor variations in some plays. These structural divisions are noted in the summaries of the plays in these Notes, but it should be remembered that such notation is artificial and is inserted only for illustrative purposes, since Greek tragedy was performed without intermissions or breaks.

The following are the main elements of a typical tragedy:

Prologue — the opening scene, in which the background of the story is established, usually by a single actor or in a dialogue between two actors.

Parodos — the entrance of the chorus, usually chanting a lyric which bears some relation to the main theme of the play.

Episode — the counterpart of the modern act or scene, in which the plot is developed through action and dialogue between the actors, with the chorus sometimes playing a minor role.

Stasimon — the choral ode. A *stasimon* comes at the end of each *episode* so that the tragedy is a measured alternation between these two elements.

Exodos — the final action after the last *stasimon,* ended by the ceremonial exit of all the players.

ARISTOTLE ON TRAGEDY

In the *Poetics,* his famous study of Greek dramatic art, Aristotle (384-322 B.C.) compares tragedy to such other metrical forms as comedy and epic. He determines that tragedy, like all poetry, is a kind of imitation (*mimesis*), but adds that it has a serious purpose and uses direct action rather than narrative to achieve its ends. He says that poetic *mimesis* is imitation of things as they could be, not as they are — i.e., of universals and ideals — thus poetry is a more philosophical and exalted medium than history, which merely records what has actually happened.

The aim of tragedy, he writes, is to bring about a "catharsis" of the spectators — to arouse in them sensations of pity and fear, and to purge them of these emotions so that they leave the theater feeling cleansed and uplifted, with a heightened understanding of the ways of gods and men. This catharsis is brought about by witnessing some disastrous and moving change in the fortunes of the drama's protagonist (Aristotle recognized that the change might not be disastrous, but felt this was the kind shown in the best tragedies — *Oedipus at Colonus,* for example, was considered a tragedy by the Greeks but does not have an unhappy ending).

According to Aristotle, tragedy has six main elements — plot, character, diction, thought, spectacle (scenic effect), and song (music), of which the first two are primary. Most of the *Poetics* is devoted to analysis of the scope and proper use of these elements, with illustrative examples selected from many tragic dramas, especially those of Sophocles, although Aeschylus, Euripides, and some playwrights whose works no longer survive are also cited.

Several of Aristotle's main points are of great value for an understanding of Greek tragic drama. Particularly significant is his statement that the plot is the most important element of tragedy. He explains —

> ...tragedy is an imitation, not of men, but of action and life, of happiness and misery. And life consists of action, and

its end is a mode of activity, not a quality. Now character determines men's qualities, but it is their action that makes them happy or wretched. The purpose of action in the tragedy, therefore, is not the representation of character: character comes in as contributing to the action. Hence the incidents and the plot are the end of the tragedy; and the end is the chief thing of all. Without action there cannot be a tragedy; there may be one without character.... The plot, then, is the first principle, and, as it were, the soul of a tragedy: character holds the second place.

Aristotle goes on to discuss the structure of the ideal tragic plot and spends several chapters on its requirements. He says that the plot must be a complete whole — with a definite beginning, middle, and end — and its length should be such that the spectators can comprehend without difficulty both its separate parts and its overall unity. Moreover, the plot requires a single central theme in which all the elements are logically related to demonstrate the change in the protagonist's fortunes, with emphasis on the dramatic causation and probability of the events.

Aristotle has relatively less to say about the tragic hero because the incidents of tragedy are often beyond the hero's control or not closely related to his personality. The plot is intended to illustrate matters of cosmic rather than individual significance and the protagonist is viewed primarily as the character who experiences the changes which take place. This stress placed by the Greek tragedians on the development of plot and action at the expense of character, and their general lack of interest in exploring psychological motivation, is one of the major differences between ancient and modern drama.

Since the aim of a tragedy is to arouse pity and fear through an alteration in the status of the central character, he must be a figure with whom the audience can identify and whose fate can trigger these emotions. Aristotle says that "pity is aroused by unmerited misfortune, fear by the misfortune of a man like ourselves." He surveys various possible types of characters on the basis of these premises, then defines the ideal protagonist as —

...a man who is highly renowned and prosperous, but one who is not pre-eminently virtuous and just, whose misfortune, however, is brought upon him not by vice or depravity but by some error of judgment or frailty; a personage like Oedipus....

In addition, the hero should not offend the moral sensibilities of the spectators, and as a character he must be true to type, true to life, and consistent.

The hero's error or frailty *(harmartia)* is often misleadingly explained as his "tragic flaw," in the sense of that personal quality which inevitably causes his downfall or subjects him to retribution. However, overemphasis on a search for the decisive flaw in the protagonist as the key factor for understanding the tragedy can lead to superficial or false interpretations. It gives more attention to personality than the dramatists intended and ignores the broader philosophical implications of the typical plot's denouement. It is true that the hero frequently takes a step which initiates the events of the tragedy and, owing to his own ignorance or poor judgment, acts in such a way as to bring about his own downfall. In a more sophisticated philosophical sense though, the hero's fate, despite its immediate cause in his finite act, comes about because of the nature of the cosmic moral order and the role played by chance or destiny in human affairs. Unless the conclusions of most tragedies are interpreted on this level, the reader is forced to credit the Greeks (and himself, by implication) with the most primitive of moral systems.

It is worth noting that some scholars believe the "flaw" was intended by Aristotle as a necessary corollary of his requirement that the hero should not be a completely admirable man. *Harmartia* would thus be the factor that delimits the protagonist's imperfection and keeps him on a human plane, making it possible for the audience to sympathize with him. This view tends to give the "flaw" an ethical definition, but relates it only to the spectators' reaction to the hero and does not increase its importance for interpreting the tragedies.

The remainder of the *Poetics* is given over to examination of the other elements of tragedy, and discussion of various techniques, devices, and stylistic principles. Aristotle mentions two features of the plot, both of which are related to the concept of *harmartia*, as crucial components of any well-made tragedy. These are "reversal" (*peripeteia*), where the opposite of what was planned or hoped for by the protagonist takes place, as when Oedipus' investigation of the murder of Laius leads to a catastrophic and unexpected conclusion; and "recognition" (*anagnorisis*), the point when the protagonist recognizes the truth of a situation, discovers another character's identity, or comes to a realization about himself. This sudden acquisition of knowledge or insight by the hero arouses the desired intense emotional reaction in the spectators, as when Oedipus finds out his true parentage and realizes what crimes he has been responsible for.

Aristotle wrote the *Poetics* nearly a century after the greatest Greek tragedians had already died, in a period when there had been radical transformations in nearly all aspects of Athenian society and culture. The tragic drama of his day was not the same as that of the fifth century, and to a certain extent his work must be construed as a historical study of a genre that no longer existed rather than as a description of a living art form.

In the *Poetics* Aristotle used the same analytical methods that he had successfully applied in studies of politics, ethics, and the natural sciences, in order to determine tragedy's fundamental principles of composition and content. This approach is not completely suited to a literary study and it is sometimes too artificial or formula-prone in its conclusions.

Nonetheless, the *Poetics* is the only critical study of Greek drama to have been made by a near-contemporary. It contains much valuable information about the origins, methods, and purposes of tragedy, and to a degree shows us how the Greeks themselves reacted to their theater. In addition, Aristotle's work had an overwhelming influence on the development of drama long after it was compiled. The ideas and principles of the *Poetics* are reflected in the drama of the Roman Empire and dominated the composition of tragedy in western Europe during the seventeenth, eighteenth, and nineteenth centuries.

THE LIFE OF AESCHYLUS

With the beginning of the fifth century B.C., the city of Athens entered the most glorious era of her history. The tyranny of Peisistratus had been overthrown in 510, and a few years later there were important political reforms resulting in a complete democracy, the first in Europe. The Persian invasion took place in 480 B.C. and, by what then seemed to be an act of God, the massed power of Asia was defeated by a coalition of the tiny Greek city-states under Athenian leadership. After this Athens organized the Delian League and began slowly to transform it into an empire. The city became wealthy and powerful, the cultural and intellectual center of all Greece. The century opened by these events was marked throughout by an energetic enterprise and a flowering of genius in all areas of human activity that has rarely been paralleled in the thousands of years since.

Aeschylus, who was born in 525 B.C., lived through these stirring events and shared the pride of all Athenians in the achievements of their city. In a sense Aeschylus was a founding father of this new Athens, for he was one of the famed "Men of Marathon," the gallant band who threw back the first wave of the Persian hordes. His dramatic works, his ideas, his philosophical attitudes, are all examples of the creativity inspired by the Athenian golden age.

Aeschylus was the son of a prominent aristocratic family in which the composition of tragic poetry was a traditional craft. He was raised in Eleusis, a small town just outside Athens that was the center of an important religious cult. In 490 B.C. he fought as an infantryman at Marathon, and ten years later, during the great invasion, took part in the naval battle at Salamis and other military actions.

Aeschylus was evidently young when he began to write tragedy. The earliest known performance of his work was at the dramatic festival of 499 B.C., but it was not until 485 that he won first prize in the annual competition. In all, Aeschylus wrote nearly 90 plays, of which seven still survive. He was victorious at the festival thirteen times (i.e., for 52 plays).

Aeschylus was responsible for several very important innovations which had a decisive influence on the development of drama. The most significant of these was his introduction of a second actor, for there had been only a single actor and the chorus available in the past. One critic has written, "The addition of another actor did not double the resources of tragedy, rather it increased them fiftyfold. To bring two opposed or sympathetic characters face to face, to exhibit the clash of principles by the clash of personalities, this is a step forward into a new world, a change so great that to call Aeschylus the very inventor of tragedy is not unreasonable." In addition, Aeschylus reduced the size of the chorus from fifty to twelve members and increased the use of dialogue in his plays. All these changes gave a greater flexibility to tragedy and vastly increased the dramatic possibilities of what was until then primarily a choral medium.

Aeschylus was also renowned for the magnificence of his poetic diction, which surpassed that of all his contemporaries, and for the elaborate staging and pageantry of his productions (a good example of this is the colorful spectacle of Agamemnon's homecoming in *The Oresteia*). His works indicate that he was an ardent patriot and a firm believer in the Athenian democracy. He was also a serious religious thinker. In his hands the old myths became powerful expressions of crucial moral and theological problems. Imbued with the confident spirit of fifth-century Athens, Aeschylus wrote tragedies that were paeans of faith in the benevolence of the universe and the perfectibility of man.

Few details of his life are still remembered, and most of them serve mainly to whet the curiosity. Aeschylus was married and had two sons, Euphorion and Bion, both of whom carried on the family tradition of writing tragedy. At the dramatic festival of 468, Aeschylus was defeated by Sophocles, who was then at the beginning of his career, but nothing else is known about this event. There is also a story that Aeschylus was very bitter when defeated by the poet Simonides in a competition to write an epitaph for the soldiers who fell at Marathon.

Aside from his military service, Aeschylus left Athens only twice, both times to visit the Greek towns on the island of Sicily.

On his first trip, around 476 B.C., he was the personal guest of the tyrant of Syracuse and lived at the royal palace. While there he wrote a tragedy in honor of the foundation of a new city on the slopes of Mount Etna.

On his second trip, shortly after the performance of *The Oresteia* in 456, Aeschylus died. According to a story current in ancient times, he had been sitting on a hillside near the town of Gela when an eagle flew by with a tortoise in its beak, searching for something hard on which to break the shell. Mistaking Aeschylus' bald head for a rock, the eagle dropped the tortoise, crushing his skull and killing him instantly.

Aeschylus was buried in Sicily. An epitaph he had written for himself was inscribed on his grave. In it the tragedian whose life had been filled with dramatic victories and the acclaim of his fellow citizens revealed the experience of which he was most proud —

> Under this monument lies Aeschylus the Athenian,
> Euphorion's son, who died in the wheatlands of
>   Gela. The grove
> of Marathon with its glories can speak of his valor
>   in battle.
> The long-haired Persian remembers and can speak
>   of it too.
>   (trans. Richard Lattimore)

A few years later a bronze statue of Aeschylus was erected in the Theater of Dionysus at Athens. In recognition of the special place he had in the development of tragedy, the people of Athens made a rule permitting the works of Aeschylus to be performed at the dramatic festivals in competition with those of living poets. As a result, the tragedies of Aeschylus were produced often and won many additional victories after his death. His works became a standard by which all later tragedies were judged and against which all later dramatists were forced to measure themselves.

In the next hundred years the Greek world underwent radical transformations and in many important respects Athens ceased to resemble the city known and loved by Aeschylus. Tastes and ideas changed. Some began to regard the language of Aeschylean tragedy as archaic. Others thought the style of his tragedies was heavy-handed and artificial. The great religious and patriotic themes that lay behind his plays sometimes seemed shallow or irrelevant. But despite these challenges, Aeschylus was always looked upon as an almost superhuman master from the dimly remembered, glorious past. He was the legendary giant of tragic poetry; often criticized or parodied, but never ignored and never forgotten. Even today Aeschylus is still respected as the first and greatest of tragedians.

EXTANT DRAMATIC WORKS OF AESCHYLUS

The Suppliants — probably the earliest surviving tragedy by Aeschylus and thus the earliest extant drama in western literature, it probably dates from around 490 B.C., although there is some evidence to indicate that it may actually have been written as late as 468 B.C. *The Suppliants* is the first play of a tetralogy which also included *The Egyptians* and *The Daughters of Danaus,* and the satyr-play *Amymone.* It was based on the legends about the fifty daughters of Danaus, who were descendants of Zeus and Io, a mortal woman, and the establishment of the family of Danaus as the royal house of Argos. *The Suppliants* is of particular interest to literary historians because it seems to represent a stage of development halfway between the choral dithyramb and conventional tragedy — the chorus of fifty maidens is the central character of the tragedy, about half the play consists of choral lyrics and much of the remaining dialogue is spoken by the chorus, the story has little action, the characterization and use of the actors is very limited.

The Persians — part of a tetralogy that was first performed at the dramatic festival of 472 B.C. and won first prize, the choregus for this production was the famous Athenian statesman Pericles. The names of the other plays in the tetralogy are known, but they seem to bear no relation to the theme of *The Persians,* indicating that the dramatic trilogy was beginning to lose its organic quality even in the time of Aeschylus. *The Persians* is the only extant Greek tragedy on a contemporary subject, for it is an exaltation of the great Athenian naval victory over the Persians at Salamis in

480 B.C. The story is told from the Persian point of view, all the characters are non-Greek, and the setting is the exotic and remote royal court of Persia. Thus, despite its historical subject the tragedy is detached from real life and has an almost mythological quality. The plot of *The Persians* reveals much adaptation and telescoping of historical events in order to illustrate clearly the moral theme that retribution comes to those mortals who are guilty of insolent pride and excessive prosperity.

The Seven Against Thebes —part of a tetralogy based on the Theban cycle of legends that was first performed at the dramatic festival of 467 B.C. and won first prize. The other tragedies in the tetralogy were entitled *Laius* and *Oedipus,* the satyr-play was *The Sphinx.* *The Seven Against Thebes* tells the story of the civil war between Eteocles and Polyneices, the sons of Oedipus, after their father's death. This same story is told in *The Phoenissae* of Euripides. Three plays by Sophocles, *King Oedipus, Oedipus at Colonus,* and *Antigone,* as well as other plays by Euripides, are based on incidents in the same cycle of legends, for it was one of the most popular in ancient times.

Prometheus Bound —first performed *ca.* 465 B.C., part of a trilogy that also included *Prometheus the Fire-Bringer* and *Prometheus Unbound.* This tragedy is based on the legend about the conflict between Zeus and the titan Prometheus, in the period just after the Olympian gods began to rule over the world. The entire trilogy probably explored such philosophical questions as the nature of god, the disharmony between the rule of force and the rule of reason, and the meaning of justice and order. These themes as treated by Aeschylus influenced many later writers, and the legend has become archetypal in western literature. The most famous work it has inspired is *Prometheus Unbound* by the English poet Shelley.

The Oresteia Trilogy (Agamemnon, The Libation Bearers, The Eumenides) —first performed at the dramatic festival of 458 B.C., won first prize. The satyr-play which completed the tetralogy was entitled *Proteus.* It dealt with the visit of Menelaus to Egypt on his way home from Troy after his ship was blown off-course by the storm mentioned in *Agamemnon*. *The Oresteia* is the only complete trilogy that still survives. See the summaries of the individual plays for detailed comments.

Aeschylus is known to have written more than eighty plays. In addition to these seven tragedies, there are still in existence a few hundred fragments of other works, ranging in size up to several lines.

THE MYTHOLOGICAL BACKGROUND

A generation before the Trojan War, two brothers, Atreus and Thyestes, contended for the throne of Argos. Thyestes seduced his brother's wife and was driven out of Argos by Atreus, who then established himself as sole king. Eventually Thyestes returned and asked to be forgiven. Atreus pretended to be reconciled with his brother, but secretly planned to avenge the seduction of his wife and at the same time to eliminate a rival for the crown by rendering Thyestes unclean in the eyes of the citizens of Argos. Atreus murdered the two young sons of Thyestes, cut their bodies into unrecognizable pieces, and had them served to their father at a banquet given in honor of his return. Thyestes was horrified when he learned what he had dined on. He cursed Atreus and all his descendants, and fled from Argos with his only remaining child, the infant Aegisthus.

When Atreus died, the throne of Argos was inherited by his son Agamemnon, who married Clytaemestra, the daughter of the king of Sparta. They had three children—Iphigenia, Electra, and Orestes. The other son of Atreus, Menelaus, married Helen, the sister of Clytaemestra, and in due course became the king of Sparta when her father died.

Most of the Greek chieftains had been among the suitors of Helen, for she was renowned to be the most beautiful woman in the world. They had made a pact to accept without protest her choice of a husband and to come to his aid if anyone attempted to steal Helen from him. Some time after Helen and Menelaus were married, Paris, the son of the king of Troy, came to Sparta. He seduced Helen and carried her back with him to Troy. Faithful to their oaths, the chieftains rallied with their armies to the call of Menelaus. A great force was mobilized to capture Troy and restore Helen to her rightful husband. Agamemnon, as leader of the largest contingent, was made commander.

The expedition assembled at Aulis, on the eastern coast of Greece, but was unable to sail for Troy because of adverse winds. Calchas, a soothsayer who accompanied the army, declared that the goddess Artemis was responsible and could only be appeased by the sacrifice of Agamemnon's daughter Iphigenia. Agamemnon was appalled by this command and refused to obey, but finally gave in to the pressure put on him by the other chieftains. He induced Clytaemestra to send Iphigenia to Aulis by claiming that the maiden was to be married to Achilles, the greatest of the Greek heroes. When the young girl arrived at the camp, however, she was sacrificed to the goddess. After this the wind changed. The army boarded its ships and set sail for Troy.

Meanwhile, Aegisthus returned to Argos in the absence of Agamemnon. He began to plot against his cousin in the hope of regaining what he considered to be his rightful place on the throne, and of avenging the treatment his father and brothers received at the hands of Atreus. Aegisthus discovered that Clytaemestra had developed a bitter hatred for Agamemnon because of the sacrifice of her daughter. Her enmity for her husband continued to increase as she received reports of his infidelity with other women while on campaign at Troy. Before long Aegisthus and Clytaemestra became lovers. They shared the same hatred for Agamemnon and began to conspire together. They planned to murder him when he came back to Argos.

The siege of Troy lasted ten years. Finally the city fell and was sacked by the Greek army, its temples were destroyed, and the surviving inhabitants were sold into slavery. The first play of the trilogy, *Agamemnon*, takes place in Argos shortly after the fall of Troy.

Agamemnon returns home with only one ship because his fleet was scattered by a storm at sea. He is accompanied by his newest concubine, Cassandra, the daughter of the king of Troy. Aegisthus remains in the background while Clytaemestra gives her husband an affectionate welcome and the people of Argos applaud their victorious king. Later, Clytaemestra traps Agamemnon in his bath and kills him with an axe. Cassandra is murdered also. Clytaemestra and Aegisthus announce the murders to the people, overcome the opposition of the Elders, and set themselves up as the new rulers of Argos.

The action of *The Choephori,* the second play, takes place a few years later. Orestes, the son of Agamemnon, has been living in exile in the nearby kingdom of Phocis. In obedience to a command given him by the god Apollo, Orestes returns to Argos to avenge his father. He seeks out his sister Electra, then gains admittance to the palace by disguising himself and kills Clytaemestra and Aegisthus. Orestes tries to justify the murder of his mother, but in the final scene of the play he is afflicted with madness and flees in terror from the Furies, hideous spirits who hunt down and punish murderers.

The story of *The Eumenides,* the last play, begins a few days later. Orestes seeks refuge in the sanctuary of Apollo at Delphi. He is forced to wander as an outcast for the next few years, with the Furies constantly tormenting him. Finally he arrives at Athens and throws himself on the mercy of the goddess Athene. The Furies follow him there and insist that Orestes must be punished for matricide. He claims that he acted according to Apollo's dictate and is not responsible for the crime. Athene convenes a special court to hear the case, but the jurors are unable to reach a verdict. Athene casts the deciding vote and Orestes is acquitted. The Furies angrily threaten vengeance on Athens, but Athene propitiates them by the offer of a position of honor in the cult of her city. They accept. The ancient Furies are transformed into benevolent spirits. Their name is changed to the Eumenides, or "kindly ones," to symbolize their new character.

The legends about the family of Atreus were among the most popular in the Greek mythological heritage and many versions of them were known in the ancient world. Some elements of the story are recounted in the *Odyssey* of Homer. Pindar and other poets made use of the legend also, and it provided the plots for many tragedies in addition to the trilogy by Aeschylus, including *Electra* by Sophocles, and *Electra, Orestes, Iphigenia at Aulis,* and *Iphigenia in Tauris* by Euripides. A complete account of the legend, with reference to all its sources and variant versions, will be found in Volume II of *The Greek Myths* by Robert Graves, available in paperback edition, or in any other good handbook of classical mythology.

THE ORESTEIA

Introductory Note

At the beginning of the fifth century, it was customary for each of the tragedians who were competing at the festival of Dionysus to present a trilogy of three plays on a related theme, followed by a satyr-play. *The Oresteia* is the only surviving example of a Greek tragic trilogy and thus has great importance in the history of drama.

Each play of the trilogy is a self-contained dramatic unit, although the endings of the first two plays lead naturally into the plays that follow them. Any of the three plays can be presented alone without too much loss of understanding, but the meaning and dramatic effect of the works is enhanced by production or reading of them as a group.

Each play has its own chorus and a nearly separate cast of characters, but the trilogy is given unity by the basis of its plots in the same cycle of legends. In addition, there are certain underlying themes that continue from play to play, and which reach their full resolution only at the conclusion of *The Eumenides*.

The main idea of *The Oresteia* is that injustice and such primitive instruments of morality as the blood-feud must be eliminated if human society is ever to attain to a high level of social organization, and this can only be done by the introduction of a public morality and civic legal processes. A compromise must be reached between those old ideas that are good and those new ideas that are good. The city of Athens, whose patron goddess is the spirit of wisdom, is exalted as the model which men ought to emulate.

The Oresteia uses the legend of the family of Atreus as raw material for examination of different aspects of this theme: such questions as the nature of justice, methods of establishing and maintaining justice on earth, the relationship of justice to vengeance, mercy, the gods, fate, and the social order. It also deals with the related doctrines that wisdom can be learned only through experience and suffering, that one crime invariably leads to another if the criminal is not punished, that blood, once shed, can never be atoned for, and that authority is the foundation of civilization.

AGAMEMNON

CHARACTERS

A Watchman
Clytaemestra, the wife of Agamemnon
A Herald
Agamemnon, the king of Argos and leader of the
    Greek expedition to Troy
Cassandra, the prophetess daughter of King Priam
    of Troy, now Agamemnon's concubine
Aegisthus, Agamemnon's cousin and hereditary
    enemy, Clytaemestra's lover
Chorus of Elders of Argos

SCENE

In front of the palace of Agamemnon at Argos

PROLOGUE (Lines 1-39)

Summary

The play opens with a watchman standing on the roof of the palace. He explains that Clytaemestra has ordered him to keep a lookout each night for the light from a series of beacon fires that will signal the long-awaited fall of Troy. He has carried out this duty faithfully for several years already and is getting demoralized. Suddenly he observes a beacon burning in the distance and realizes that the war is over. The watchman is excited for a moment by the happy thought that his long vigil is ended and that his king will finally return home, but then a feeling of gloom comes over him. He refuses to state aloud the cause of his foreboding, but remarks that the walls of the palace could tell the story if they were able to speak. The watchman determines to remain silent. He will be satisfied to welcome his beloved king home again. He goes out to tell the news to Clytaemestra.

Comment

The watchman's speech sets the gloomy, tense mood that will be maintained throughout the play. There is skillful artistry evident in this powerful opening and full use is made of dramatic irony. Moreover, the watchman has been made into a real man instead of a mechanical giver of information. His ambiguous reaction and brooding thoughts are genuine in the circumstances. They immediately arouse the interest of the audience and give added poignancy to his guarded comments.

PARODOS (Lines 40-82)

The Chorus of Argive Elders enter. The old men say that ten years have passed since Agamemnon and his brother Menelaus sailed to Troy with their army. Zeus ordained that a bloody war be fought to avenge the seduction of Helen by Paris. Many men have already suffered and died "for one woman's promiscuous sake," and the war still goes on. The elders add that they were too old and weak to serve in the expedition to Troy.

FIRST STASIMON (Lines 83-269)

Summary

Clytaemestra comes out of the palace. The elders ask why she has ordered sacrifices to be offered at all the altars in the city. Before she is able to answer, they repeat the story of a portent that was observed when Agamemnon and his army left Argos. Two giant eagles attacked and ripped apart a pregnant hare, killing her and her unborn young. Calchas, the soothsayer, claimed that the eagles represented Agamemnon and Menelaus, while the hare was a symbol of Troy; thus the omen was a sign of victory. Calchas added that Artemis, the virgin goddess of hunting, might become angered at Zeus because his eagles had destroyed the hare, her sacred animal. He warned that Artemis might seek vengeance by demanding a sacrifice from Agamemnon. If he refused, she would prevent the Greek fleet from sailing to Troy, in an effort to thwart the will of Zeus.

The elders ponder on the suffering that so often seems to accompany divine intervention in human affairs. The problem is a perplexing one that cannot be solved, although it is known that Zeus has ultimate responsibility for all that happens. They conclude, "From the gods who sit in grandeur/ grace comes somehow violent."

Resuming their story, the elders tell how the Greek fleet was unable to sail from Aulis, the assembly place of the expedition, because of adverse winds sent by Artemis. Calchas told Agamemnon that it would be necessary for him to sacrifice his daughter Iphigenia to placate the angry goddess. Agamemnon and the other chieftains were horrified by this advice. Agamemnon was faced by a terrible dilemma, for he had conflicting sacred obligations to his family and his army, and whichever decision he made was bound to be sinful. Finally, "when necessity's yoke was put upon him," Agamemnon chose to ignore his feelings as a father. Iphigenia, an innocent maiden, was slaughtered on the altar. The pitiful scene tore the hearts of all who were present. Shortly afterward the wind changed and the fleet sailed for Troy.

The elders disapprove of Agamemnon's decision. They say that his mind was warped by lust for power and prestige, and warn that "Justice so moves that those only learn who suffer...." They turn to Clytaemestra and repeat their question, asking the reason for the sacrifices.

Comment

In *Agamemnon* the *parodos* is followed immediately by the
first *stasimon;* both together constitute one of the longest lyrical
passages in all Greek tragedy. The story told by the chorus helps
to clarify some of the allusions in the watchman's speech, although
the elders seem to have many of the same ambiguous feelings. The
choral account of the events before the expedition to Troy is a
reminder of the curse on the House of Atreus, for the sacrifice of
Iphigenia is an example of how one crime breeds another and provides a history of sinfulness for which Agamemnon must eventually
be punished. It is worth noting that Agamemnon freely made the
decision to sacrifice his daughter. Fate and the curse circumscribed
his choice, but the final responsibility for Iphigenia's death and his
own downfall is his.

The choral passage on Zeus is an attempt to justify the ways of
God to man and introduces one of the main philosophical ideas
of the trilogy—that wisdom is learned through suffering and that
affairs on earth are controlled by the divine will. There are many
mysteries that man cannot solve, but God is the source of all
things. It is possible that Aeschylus viewed the gods of the Olympian pantheon as symbols of some kind, for here he seems to see
one god, "Zeus: whatever he may be," as the primary moral power
in the universe.

FIRST EPISODE (Lines 270-366)

Summary

Clytaemestra informs the elders that Troy has fallen. They
accept this news doubtfully and ask for proof. She tells them about
the system of beacons on hilltops and islands between Troy and
Argos that she arranged with Agamemnon and gives a vivid description of how the news reached her.

Clytaemestra gives free rein to her imagination and goes on
to describe the situation in the conquered city. She visualizes the
Greek army looting and pillaging in the ruins of Troy while the
defeated inhabitants mourn. Clytaemestra points out that the

voyage home is long and dangerous, and expresses the hope that the Greeks have not committed any sacrilege in Troy that would offend the gods.

Comment

The first speech of Clytaemestra is particularly appropriate after the story of the sacrifice of Iphigenia, for she is the human embodiment of the bitterness and wrath engendered by the sacrifice and the curse that lies behind it. Clytaemestra is a majestic and powerful woman whose personality dominates the whole tragedy. She is the only character to appear in all three plays of the trilogy. Aeschylus is not too interested in her psychological motivation, however, because his drama is based on the conflict and interplay of important ethical and philosophical principles rather than the emotional development of an individual. His portrayal of Clytaemestra is strikingly human, but he does not explore her thoughts or feelings to any great extent.

In this scene the strength of Clytaemestra's character is shown by her ease in convincing the elders that her news is true, and by the "masculine" efficiency with which she arranged the complicated system of beacons. Clytaemestra's hope that the conquering Greeks will not be guilty of impiety can be read in several ways — it is a conventional expression intended to delude the chorus, but it may also indicate that she hopes nothing will interfere with Agamemnon's return so that she will not lose her chance for revenge, and that she really does hope the Greeks will offend the gods, for then she will have divine sanction when she kills their leader. Such complex meanings are typical of all Clytaemestra's main speeches. They emphasize her audacious subtlety, for she is so proud and confident that she is not afraid to hint at her plans, and they also heighten the dramatic irony of many scenes.

SECOND STASIMON (Lines 367-480)

Summary

The elders attribute Troy's fall to the wrath of Zeus. He always punishes mortal impiety and pride, and Paris sinned by violating the sacred obligations of a guest when he kidnaped Helen from Mene-laus. But he was repaid, for the dowry that Helen brought to Paris and the Trojans was death. A terrible war took place in which Greeks as well as Trojans suffered. This war has dragged on for many years and the people of Argos are restive. Their sons and husbands are gone. Every ship brings back the ashes of more dead soldiers. All this hardship has been endured for the sake of a worth-less woman, but now the Argives are bitter and war-weary. The elders fear that Agamemnon will be punished for inflicting this burden on his people. The gods, they say, take note of those who are responsible for bloodshed and punish them. The only security is to avoid fame and power.

Comment

The images of this ode foreshadow the death of Agamemnon and the sorrows that will continue to afflict the House of Atreus (e.g., the description of Zeus casting the net of destruction over Troy also alludes to how Clytaemestra will trap Agamemnon in a net before killing him). The story of the horrors brought down on Troy because of Paris' sin is meant to parallel the story of the destructive forces brought into action by Agamemnon's sacrifice of his daughter. The main point of the ode is that retribution comes to all sinners. This universal moral law applies as well to Agamem-non as it does to Priam and the Trojans, although only Troy is used as an example. The *stasimon* begins as a hymn of joy on the down-fall of Troy, but ends as a tacit condemnation of Agamemnon and a hint that worse things are still in store.

The portion of the ode beginning, "The god of war, money changer of dead bodies," is one of the most famous lyrics written by Aeschylus. It is a simple but moving description of the horrors of war. One critic has said of it, "no greater lyric poetry than this has survived from ancient Greece."

SECOND EPISODE (Lines 481-685)

Summary

Several days have gone by. The elders chatter excitedly to-gether about the rumors that are spreading through the news-starved city, now that everyone knows that the war is over. They begin to doubt Clytaemestra's information and suspect that she has been guilty of feminine impetuosity in announcing the war's end.

At this moment a herald enters bringing definite news that the war is over. Agamemnon and the army have just landed on the beach below the city and he has been sent ahead with the message. The herald tells the elders of his happiness at being home again and describes the hardships that the army endured during the long siege. He gives an unromantic and bitter account of the war, then tells about the destruction of Troy and mentions that the temples of the fallen city were desecrated by the victorious army.

The elders welcome the herald and express joy at his news. They hint that affairs in Argos are in bad order and hope that the returning soldiers will solve the city's problems, but the herald does not understand what they mean.

Clytaemestra steps forward and mocks the Chorus for having doubted her. She claims to be gratified by Agamemnon's safe return and gives the herald a message for her husband, welcoming him home and announcing that she will give him a triumphal reception when he enters the city. Clytaemestra adds ironically, "may he find a wife within his house as true/ as on the day he left her...." and praises her own fidelity to Agamemnon.

After Clytaemestra exits, the herald tells the elders about the fate of Menelaus. The fleet encountered a violent storm on its return voyage. The ships were scattered and many went down during the tempest. In fact, Agamemnon has reached Argos with only one ship of his whole contingent. Menelaus is still missing, but the herald is certain that he will get home safely. He leaves to deliver Clytaemestra's message to Agamemnon.

Comment

The herald's message confirms the fall of Troy, but his offhand admission that the Greek conquerors were guilty of sacrilege heightens the general tension. The elders sense that something is wrong, but are reluctant to speak openly because they have just

been humiliated by Clyaemestra after the herald's arrival. Clytaemestra's message to Agamemnon is filled with double meanings and
veiled threats that are comprehensible only to the audience.

The long digression about Menelaus is important because his
absence will make it easier for Clytaemestra and Aegisthus to
murder Agamemnon and take over the state. It also provides the
theme for *Proteus,* the satyr-play that followed the *Oresteia* trilogy.

THIRD STASIMON (Lines 686-773)

Summary

The chorus chants an ode on Helen and the destruction caused
by her beauty. Helen's very name means "death," they say, and it
is appropriate for one who was responsible for so much devastation.
At first the Trojans welcomed her, but they regretted their gener-
osity when the war began. The elders tell a parable to illustrate
what happened. Once a man raised a lion cub in his house. In the
beginning it was a source of pleasure for him and his family. Later,
when the cub grew up, its destructive instincts became dominant.
The lion ravened ferociously among the man's sheep, then attacked
the defenseless family. "This thing they raised in their house was
blessed/ by God to be priest of destruction." Thus it was with
Helen — whatever she touched was destroyed.

Many people believe that good fortune results in suffering, but
the elders hold another view — only evil deeds result in evil. Those
who do not sin are not punished, but evil breeds more evil. Insolence
and arrogant pride are resented by the gods and bring down retribution on man. The blessings of happiness are given to the righteous —
those who value honor and justice and lead humble lives.

Comment

These verses preceding the entrance of Agamemnon are made
up of reflections on sin, retribution, and justice, all illustrated by
reference to the fate of the Trojans. These moral laws are universal,
however, and apply also to Agamemnon. No one can escape the
wrath of the gods if he has sinned. Agamemnon is already guilty

of serious misdeeds and in the next scene he will commit one last great sin. This ode is thus a prediction and explanation of his downfall.

THIRD EPISODE (Lines 774-965)

Summary

Agamemnon makes a triumphal entry in a chariot. Cassandra is at his side and they are accompanied by attendants.

The elders greet their king with a frank statement intended to avoid superfluous praise yet give him the honor to which he is entitled. They remind Agamemnon of their opposition to the war, but express genuine pleasure that he is home again. The elders add that Agamemnon will soon learn who has been loyal and who disloyal during his absence.

Agamemnon states that he will offer thanks to all the gods of Argos for his safe return and for their aid in conquering Troy. Everything that happens on earth, he says, is determined by the gods. Men must always remember to praise and thank them for their assistance. After the sacrifice, Agamemnon continues, he will act in accordance with the advice given by the elders and will convene an assembly of the people to settle all disputes and end dissension before trouble arises. The good elements in the state will be strengthened; the rest will be purged.

Clytaemestra tells the elders that she is not ashamed to declare her love for Agamemnon in their presence and steps forward to greet her husband. She tells him about the hardships that a wife must undergo while her husband is away at war—there are constant worries, rumors that he has been killed or wounded. Many times these fears caused terrible nightmares or drove her to the verge of suicide. Clytaemestra was so afraid that Agamemnon would be killed at Troy or that the unrest at home would result in rebellion, she says, that she sent their son Orestes to stay with King Strophius of Phocis, where he would be safe from any danger. Clytaemestra repeats how she worried about her "beloved" Agamemnon while he was gone. She invites him to enter the palace and orders her maidens to spread a luxurious crimson tapestry on the ground for him to walk on.

Agamemnon makes a caustic reply to this effusive welcome. He tells Clytaemestra that her speech and his absence have one thing in common—they were both too long. Furthermore, he says, she is not to treat him with such extravagant praise and luxury, as if he were a depraved oriental. Such excessive splendor as spreading a tapestry on the ground to walk on is fitting only for the gods. The man who is presumptuous enough to imitate their glory is guilty of irreverence and insolence. Agamemnon concludes:

> Discordant is the murmur at such treading down
> of lovely things; while God's most lordly gift to man
> is decency of mind. Call that man only blest
> who has in sweet tranquility brought his life to close.
> If I could only act as such, my hope is good.

Clytaemestra urges Agamemnon to satisfy her desire to honor him. She coaxes him until he gives in. Agamemnon removes his sandals and, expresing the hope that the gods will not be offended, steps down onto the tapestry. Clytaemestra scornfully remarks that she would have trampled many splendors to bring Agamemnon home again. As she and her husband walk into the palace, Clytaemestra calls on Zeus to answer her prayers and help her to carry out what she plans.

Comment

This scene, with its rich tapestry, chariots, and many attendants, makes full use of visual effects, to an extent uncommon in classical tragedy. It is the only scene in which Agamemnon appears. He is a man of heroic stature and great accomplishments, but he is also conceited and pompous and this makes him vulnerable to Clytaemestra's cajoling. He is unable to understand the veiled warning given by the chorus and does not seem sincere in giving credit to the gods or his human allies for helping him to achieve his great victory at Troy. His lines about the sin of insolence seem to be a thoughtless mouthing of conventional sentiments and do not reflect any real devoutness.

This confrontation between Agamemnon and Clytaemestra is the dramatic climax of the tragedy. Clytaemestra's aim is to make Agamemnon commit one final sin, for such a disrespectful act will anger the gods against him and enlist their support for her. Agamemnon seems to dislike his wife, but he underestimates her ability and is easily susceptible to her wiles. She agilely fences with him until he has been bent to her will. His surrender is a sure sign that her plot will succeed. Clytaemestra displays almost demonic cunning in the choice of devices she uses to trap Agamemnon — endearment, flattery, servility, an attack on his courage. Her final lines are filled with exultant irony, for she knows that she will triumph, but her own downfall is also alluded to when she mentions Orestes.

FOURTH STASIMON (Lines 966-1018)

The chorus is confused. Despite the victorious homecoming of Agamemnon and Clytaemestra's warm welcome to her husband, the elders have a vague sensation of impending doom. They pray that future events will show this feeling to have been unwarranted.

FOURTH EPISODE (Lines 1019-1410)

Summary

Clytaemestra comes out of the palace and asks Cassandra to come inside with her. She promises to treat the princess with kindness, but Cassandra does not reply. Clytaemestra repeats her invitation. Cassandra continues to ignore her. Finally Clytaemestra loses her temper and goes inside again, muttering angrily.

There is a moment of silence, then Cassandra steps down from the chariot and cries out in despair that Apollo has destroyed her. The curiosity of the elders is aroused and they encourage her to continue speaking. When Cassandra realizes that she is standing outside the palace of Agamemnon, the House of Atreus, she begins to lament for herself. The elders question her. Cassandra's answers are disjointed and incoherent, but gradually her story becomes clear. She once rejected the advances of Apollo and was punished by him with the gift of prophecy. Now she is able to foretell the future, but Apollo's curse prevents anyone from believing her prophecies. The burden of being unable to communicate her vision is more painful than she can endure.

As she goes on lamenting, Cassandra enters into a prophetic ecstasy. She recounts the whole story of the curse on the House of Atreus, beginning with the feud between Atreus, the father of Agamemnon, and Thyestes, the father of Aegisthus. When Cassandra speaks about past events, the elders are able to understand and recognize that she is telling the truth. But then Apollo's curse takes effect. Cassandra is horrified by a vision of sin and bloodshed. She tries to tell the elders that Clytaemestra is about to murder Agamemnon, but they misunderstand and accuse her of lying. Cassandra realizes that there is no hope of convincing them. She becomes hysterical and foresees her own death and the coming of Orestes to avenge his father. Casting down her prophetic staff and wreath, Cassandra bravely enters the palace to meet her death.

The chorus chants a short lyric on the wickedness of prosperity. Suddenly Agamemnon's voice is heard from inside the palace, screaming that he has been stabbed. The elders mill about in confusion, wondering what course of action to follow. They are about to enter the palace when the doors swing open to reveal the dead bodies of Agamemnon and Cassandra. Clytaemestra is standing triumphantly beside the two corpses.

Comment

The result of the short confrontation between Clytaemestra and Cassandra is in striking contrast to Clytaemestra's duel with Agamemnon. By her silence the Trojan captive shows herself to be a match for the Argive queen.

Cassandra's silence contributes to a feeling of tension which explodes suddenly after Clytaemestra goes into the palace. Cassandra is a human symbol of Agamemnon's wickedness—he has slain her family, destroyed her home, and violated her in defiance of her sacred oath of chastity. Cassandra's presence underlines the reasons why the gods will allow Agamemnon to be murdered. In a long lyrical speech in which Time seems to be suspended,

Cassandra recounts the full circle of sins—past, present, future— that haunt the House of Atreus. She foresees no hope for reconciliation or an end to the curse, for she believes that all men inevitably are made to suffer at the hands of the gods. At the end of this powerful speech Cassandra accepts her own fate with dignity. Her last words—"Alas, poor men, their destiny...." generalize her tragic end into the great tragic experience of all mankind, broadening the meaning of the trilogy so that it refers to the most important problems of human religious speculation. Unlike Agamemnon, Cassandra is fully aware of her impending death. At the conclusion of this speech she enters the palace and dies in silence, while his screams echo around her.

EXODOS (Lines 1411-1673)

Summary

Clytaemestra exultingly says that now she can reveal herself and speak the truth. She tells how she trapped Agamemnon in a net as he stepped from his bath and hacked him to death with three blows of an axe. She laughed with joy as the blood from his wounds splattered her.

The elders are stunned by Clytaemestra's sadistic arrogance. She mocks them for having thought she was an ordinary, weak woman and cries defiantly:

> ...You can praise or blame me as you will;
> it is all one to me. That man is Agamemnon,
> my husband; he is dead; the work of this right hand
> that struck in strength of righteousness. And that
> is that.

The elders threaten that Clytaemestra will be banished from Argos for these murders, but she retorts that Agamemnon was not banished for the murder of Iphigenia and demands to know how they can speak of justice when they were willing to tolerate that heinous crime. Clytaemestra insists that the murder of Agamemnon was justified—partly because of the sacrifice of Iphigenia and his infidelity with Cassandra and other women while at Troy, but also because she has acted as an agent of the gods and helped to fulfill the curse on the House of Atreus.

The elders continue to lament for the dead Agamemnon and to argue with his murderess. Finally Clytaemestra manages to calm them. They still condemn her crime, but a basis for understanding has been reached because they are unable to deny her conviction that the murder was righteous. They are also reassured by her insistence that she has no intention of taking advantage of the people of Argos, now that their king is dead.

At this moment Aegisthus enters, followed by a troop of soldiers. He is happy about the death of his old enemy and gives a brief account of his grievances against Agamemnon as an additional justification for the murder.

The elders resent Aegisthus' gloating and accuse him of cowardice and effeminacy. Some heated insults are exchanged and swords are drawn. The elders, though old men, are about to engage in a fight with the soldiers of Aegisthus when Clytaemestra asserts her authority and takes control of the situation. She says there has already been enough violence and bloodshed, and urges both factions to put down their weapons.

The elders continue to defy Aegisthus, for they realize that Clytaemestra intends to share the throne with him. They warn that the citizens of Argos will rise up against him and that Orestes will return to avenge his father's murder.

Aegisthus angrily threatens to punish the elders for their insolence, but Clytaemestra advises him to ignore the impotent rantings of weak old men. After all, she says, the power in Argos is now in their hands and they will rule severely. The chorus files out and the play ends.

Comment

Clytaemestra is no longer obligated to restrain herself or conceal her inner thoughts in this final scene. She exults openly after killing her husband and shows no remorse or shame. She proudly asserts that her acts were righteous and the elders are unable to contradict her because so many ethical strands have become tangled by the tragic history of the family of Atreus. Clytaemestra also defies the threats of the chorus and asserts her control over Aegisthus and the kingdom. It can now be seen what bitterness had built up within her while Agamemnon was still alive, but she demonstrates superb poise and self-possession at the height of her triumph. The central place that Clytaemestra has held in the tragedy is emphasized by the fact that she speaks the last lines of the play, for normally this privilege was reserved for the chorus.

Agamemnon ends on a note of hostility and tension. Nothing has been resolved by the murder, for even the resolute Clytaemestra has a faint realization that the curse is as potent as ever and she will have to pay for her crime. *Agamemnon* is about murder and revenge, but the tragedy also has serious philosophical undercurrents concerning the nature of justice and the relations of men with god and with other men. Since these themes underlie the entire trilogy and are not resolved until the conclusion of *The Eumenides,* final discussion of the meaning of the *Oresteia* will be deferred until page 68.

THE CHOEPHORI, or THE LIBATION BEARERS

CHARACTERS

Orestes, the son of Agamemnon and Clytaemestra
Pylades, his friend
Electra, the sister of Orestes
A Doorkeeper
Clytaemestra, the mother of Orestes and murderess of Agamemnon, now queen of Argos
Cilissa, the nurse who cared for Orestes when he was an infant
Aegisthus, the cousin of Agamemnon and accomplice in his murder, now king of Argos
A Servant
Chorus of Captive Serving-Women

SCENE

In front of the tomb of Agamemnon

TIME

About seven years after the events in *Agamemnon*

PROLOGUE (Lines 1-21)

Summary

Orestes and Pylades enter. They are both dressed as travelers. Orestes places two locks of his hair on Agamemnon's tomb—one in honor of the river god Inachus, who watched over him in boyhood, and the other dedicated to his father, as compensation for not having been present to mourn at his funeral. Looking up, Orestes sees Electra and a group of women dressed in black approaching the tomb. Orestes utters a brief prayer to Zeus for help in avenging Agamemnon's murder; then the two young men hide, in order to observe the women and learn why they have come to the tomb.

Comment

This scene is unusually short because the first part of the *prologue* is missing in ancient manuscripts of the play. In the lost portion Orestes probably told about Apollo's command to avenge Agamemnon, since from the outset of the play Orestes seems to regard the murder of Clytaemestra as his unquestioned duty. He has come to Agamemnon's tomb to ask the dead man's spirit to assist in this undertaking and does not immediately identify himself to Electra and the women because of a prudent sense of caution.

PARODOS (Lines 22-82)

Summary

The chorus chant that they have been sent to mourn at the grave of Agamemnon by Clytaemestra because she has been tormented by bad dreams and hopes in this way to appease her dead husband's spirit. Clytaemestra believes that libations at the tomb will protect her from retribution, but, the chorus say, nothing can wash away the blood-guilt of a murder and all such crimes inevitably are punished.

Comment

The first choral ode establishes the moral and emotional background of the play by renewing the oppressive, pessimistic mood in which *Agamemnon* concluded. Despite her confident assertion that no more blood would be shed, Clytaemestra is beginning to realize that she will have to pay for her crime. Orestes, it will be seen, is not eager to kill his mother, but Apollo has commanded it and he will do his duty. It appears that the cycle of violence and murder will go on forever unless an acceptable moral solution is found.

The women of the chorus are captives, but their bitterness and desire for revenge against the murderers seems more intense than that of Orestes and Electra. This is because they are symbolic spokesmen for the primitive and absolute moral law that is responsible for the moral dilemma in the trilogy—blood must be paid for with more blood, or, in the words of the Old Testament, "an eye for an eye."

An interesting technical point here is that the details of Clytaemestra's dream are withheld until later in the play, where they will have more dramatic effect.

FIRST EPISODE (Lines 83-304)

Summary

Electra asks the women to tell her what words she ought to utter as she pours the libations, for all she can think of is bitter and inappropriate. Is she to say, for instance, that this offering is for a beloved husband from his loving wife, when she knows that Clytaemestra murdered Agamemnon? Or is she to repeat the conventional formula, asking that the spirit repay with kindness those who sent the offerings?

The women, who are still devoted to their dead master, advise her to pray for revenge against Aegisthus and Clytaemestra, and to ask her father's blessings for herself, Orestes, and all others who hate his murderers.

Electra prays to Hermes to carry her message to Agamemnon, then calls upon her father. She asks him to have pity on herself and Orestes, both deprived of their rightful inheritance and status. She is almost a slave, she says, and Orestes is exiled from his homeland, but the murderers live in freedom and luxury. Let justice triumph and the murderers be punished.

When her prayer is finished, Electra pours the libations on her father's grave. The chorus also pray at the tomb, asking for an avenger to punish those who killed Agamemnon and liberate the House of Atreus and all those, like themselves, who are forced to serve the tyrants.

Glancing around, Electra suddenly notices the two locks of hair. She examines them closely and realizes by their color and texture that they must belong to Orestes. Besides, as the chorus point out, who else would leave such a token on her father's grave? A moment later she sees a footprint in the soft ground near the tomb. She puts her own foot alongside it and discerns a marked family resemblance. It can belong to no one but Orestes, yet he is nowhere to be seen.

Electra is at her wit's end with confusion and hope when Orestes steps out from his hiding place and identifies himself. At first she is unable to believe that he is really her brother, but the locks of hair are clearly his and it was his foot that made the print she discovered. In addition he shows her a piece of cloth with a unique design that she weaved for him when he was a child. Electra realizes that her brother has finally come home again and begins to weep with joy. She tells him that he is her entire family and the sole object of all her love, for Agamemnon and her sister Iphigenia are dead and she cannot love the mother who murdered her father.

Orestes comforts and reassures his sister, then they pray to Zeus. Orestes refers to the two of them as the orphaned children of the eagle Agamemnon and asks that the king of the gods, to whom the eagle is sacred, protect and help them. He also points out that the restoration of the House of Atreus will add to the glory and majesty of Zeus.

The chorus warn Orestes to be careful, lest spies carry the news of his return to Aegisthus. Orestes is not afraid and says that Apollo will protect him. He reveals that the oracle of Apollo has ordered him to avenge his father's death and has threatened him with the most horrible torments if he fails to obey this command. As if such an oracle were not enough, Orestes says, he has compelling personal motives to drive him — his filial duty to the memory of Agamemnon, his bitterness over the loss of his inheritance, and his obligations to the people of Argos, the conquerors of Troy, who now live in shame and are tyrannized by Aegisthus and Clytaemestra.

Comment

Recognition scenes like this one involving Electra and Orestes were common features of later Greek tragedy. The recognition scene in *The Choephori* is the earliest to survive and was parodied by Euripides in his *Electra*. The circumstances of the recognition are artificial and seem a little implausible, but the scene fulfills an important function and Aeschylus was probably not concerned with achieving an effect of verisimilitude. His main interest was to bring Orestes and Electra together so that the intrigue which is the basis of the plot could get under way.

Neither Orestes nor Electra is a full character in the modern theatrical sense, for Aeschylus does not attempt to examine too deeply their psychological or emotional states. To some extent Orestes is an instrument in the hand of Apollo. He is dominated by the oracle's command and does not question his obligation to kill Clytaemestra. Some critics have said that he is meant to be a symbol of a stage in human moral evolution, but there is genuine human feeling in his characterization and Aeschylus makes a point of giving him individualized motives to supplement Apollo's dictate.

Electra does not have the importance given her in later plays on this legend by Sophocles and Euripides. She disappears after the second *stasimon* and has no role in the remaining sections of the play. Her main functions are to describe the misery and humiliation she has suffered at the hands of the murderers and to give details of the aftermath of Agamemnon's killing, all of which anger Orestes and make him more resolute. She also provides him with information about the situation in Argos that he would be unable to know otherwise, having been in exile for almost seven years.

FIRST STASIMON (Lines 305-476)

Summary

Orestes, Electra, and the chorus chant responsively a lyrical lament on the death of Agamemnon. As they describe his greatness in life, the injustice of his murder, and the humiliations his corpse and children were made to suffer at the hands of his murderers, they work themselves into a savage frenzy of rage and vengefulness.

Comment

The meaning of this long, three-sided, lyrical passage has been debated by critics. It seems to serve several functions, all aimed at creating an atmosphere in which the murder of Clytaemestra is dramatically and psychologically convincing. To some extent the scene is a mystical invocation of the spirit of Agamemnon to aid in the plot for revenge, and, at the same time, a substitute for the funeral obsequies his body never received. It is also an emotional preparation of Orestes for the murder of Clytaemestra. He is already determined to kill her because of the oracle, but the detailed account of Agamemnon's death and mutilation show him the full magnitude of the crime he is avenging. He, Electra, the chorus — and the audience also — are aroused to the savage fury necessary to condone the slaying of a mother by her son.

The motives of the participants in the plot are clearly defined in this scene. Electra is driven by personal feelings — grief for her father and despair about her own predicament. Orestes is concerned with the loss of his inheritance, the dishonor which casts a shadow over his family's name, and, most important, obedience to Apollo's command. The chorus is determined to see that the ancient law of retaliation is upheld.

SECOND EPISODE (Lines 477-582)

Summary

Orestes and Electra are now resolute in their intention to kill Clytaemestra and Aegisthus. They invoke Agamemnon's spirit one last time in a request for assistance. The chorus state their approval of Orestes' single-minded determination and urge him to take action at once.

He agrees, but first wants to know why Clytaemestra sent libations to the grave of the man whom she murdered, especially since she can never atone for his death. The chorus answer that it was because of a dream that terrified her the night before. In it Clytaemestra gave birth to a serpent. She wrapped the serpent in infant's swaddling clothes and nursed it at her breast, but it drew forth blood along with the milk.

This is no empty dream, says Orestes, but a true vision sent by his father. He hopes that he will be able to fulfill the dream and interprets the serpent to represent himself and the blood as a sign that he will kill Clytaemestra. Now, Orestes says, he must transmute his own nature and become like a serpent.

Orestes quickly lays his plans. It is necessary that those who killed by treachery must themselves be killed by treachery, for so Apollo has ordained. He tells Electra to keep his return a secret and go back to the palace where she can stay on guard for any developments that might be important. Meanwhile, he and Pylades, disguised as travelers from Phocis and speaking the Phocian dialect, will appear at the door of the palace and seek admittance. After that he will take the first opportunity that arises to kill Aegisthus and Clytaemestra. He instructs the chorus to remain silent and not to get involved unless circumstances are such that they can assist in the furtherance of his plans.

Comment

Clytaemestra's dream is a good illustration of how the poetic imagery of Aeschylus intensifies the meaning of his tragedies. In an earlier scene Orestes referred to his mother as "the deadly viper" who devoured Agamemnon. In the dream she is destroyed by a serpent, her own offspring. This is a symbolic description of the insidious and deadly hereditary curse on the House of Atreus. It is also an expression of Clytaemestra's guilty conscience and ambiguous feeling toward her son that can be meaningfully elaborated in Freudian terms.

SECOND STASIMON (Lines 583-648)

Summary

The chorus sing that the earth has many dangers — wild beasts, meteors, whirlwinds. None is more dangerous than human rashness and stubbornness, and most dangerous of all is the reckless passion of women.

There are many terrifying examples of the lengths to which women have gone when possessed by passion. Althea knew that her son Meleager could live only as long as a certain piece of wood was undamaged, but in a rage she burned the wood and killed him. Scylla caused the death of her father by cutting a sacred golden hair from his head in return for a gift given her by King Minos. The women of Lemnos joined together in a secret pact and massacred their husbands.

In the end, however, all these women were punished, for Right, aided by Destiny, always triumphs. Thus it will happen to Clytaemestra also. Even now, "Vengeance brings home at last/ a child, to wipe out the stain of blood shed long ago."

Comment

This ode serves as a decorative interlude and source of diversion and relief for the audience, but it also makes some pointed comments of great dramatic relevance to the next few scenes.

THIRD EPISODE (Lines 649-778)

Summary

The scene has changed to the outside of Agamemnon's palace at Argos. Orestes and Pylades knock at the door. A servant answers.

Orestes tells him that they are travelers with an important message and are seeking a place to stay for the night.

The servant calls Clytaemestra. She comes to the door and welcomes the strangers. After offering them the hospitality of the palace, she asks to hear their message. Orestes says that he and his companion are Daulian merchants, just arrived in Argos from Phocis. On the road to Argos they encountered Strophius, the king of Phocis, who asked them to inform the parents of Orestes that their son was dead. Clytaemestra begins to lament for the dead Orestes, then invites the two "merchants" to come inside.

A moment later Cilissa, an old woman who was Orestes' nurse when he was a child, comes out of the palace. She tells the chorus that Clytaemestra has sent her to tell the news to Aegisthus and bring him back to the palace to question the strangers. She accuses Clytaemestra of affecting grief for the sake of appearances and begins tearfully to reminisce about Orestes as an infant. The old nurse says that the news of the death is the hardest blow she has yet had to endure in her long life. She adds bitterly that Aegisthus, the defiler of the House of Atreus, will be glad to hear this sad news.

The chorus ask whether Clytaemestra's message advises Aegisthus to return to the palace accompanied by his usual body-guard of soldiers. Cilissa replies that these were Clytaemestra's instructions. The chorus tell her to withhold this part of the message so that Aegisthus will return alone. Cilissa is puzzled, but agrees to do as they ask.

Comment

Clytaemestra's warm welcome to the strangers has a special irony because it calls to mind her welcome to Agamemnon in the first play of the trilogy and this association puts her murder by Orestes into a category as morally ambiguous as her own crime. Her lament for Orestes is moving and seems genuine until Cilissa reveals that Clytaemestra's grief is false and that she is really over-joyed at the news. The self-control and fast thinking behind Clytae-mestra's pretense show that she is essentially the same woman she was in *Agamemnon*.

The naturalistic characterization of Cilissa has been praised by many critics. She has several important functions. Her sincere grief serves as a standard by which to measure Clytaemestra's affected sorrow and secret joy. There is also a striking contrast between the innocent baby described by the nurse and the unhappy man that fate has made of Orestes.

In this scene the chorus steps out of its usual role as spectator and commentator to take a part in the intrigue leading up to the killing of Aegisthus and Clytaemestra. The elimination of the soldiers who normally escort Aegisthus is an essential contribution to Orestes' success.

THIRD STASIMON (Lines 779-836)

The chorus call on Olympian Zeus and all the other gods to grant success to Orestes in his effort to avenge his father and cleanse the House of Atreus. They pray that the curse will be ended at last.

FOURTH EPISODE (Lines 837-933)

Summary

Aegisthus enters. He doubts the news of Orestes' death and is eager to interrogate the two strangers. He enters the palace. A moment later his screams are heard. A servant rushes out, shouting that Aegisthus is dead. Clytaemestra appears, hears the news, and immediately realizes that Orestes is back and has tricked her. She sends the servant to get her a weapon.

As the servant goes out, Orestes and Pylades enter with drawn swords. At last the mother and son confront each other. You are next, Orestes says. Clytaemestra orders Orestes to stand back, then appeals to him to remember that she is the mother who gave him life and raised him in infancy. Orestes hesitates in confusion and turns to Pylades for advice. His friend reminds him of Apollo's command to avenge Agamemnon and says, "Count all men hateful to you rather than the gods."

Orestes agrees that Pylades is right. He sternly orders Clytaemestra into the palace and says that he intends to kill her alongside the body of her dead lover. Clytaemestra begins to plead for mercy. She reminds Orestes that she saved his life by sending him to Phocis and claims that she was justified in killing Agamemnon. When she sees that Orestes is unswayed by this appeal, Clytaemestra warns that her curse will torment him forever if he kills her. Orestes replies that he will be tormented by his father's curse if he spares her. Clytaemestra realizes with horror that Orestes is the serpent to whom she gave birth in her dream and loses all hope. Orestes takes her by the arm and drags her into the palace.

Comment

Aeschylus has weakened Clytaemestra's defense in this scene in order to make the matricide more palatable and to prepare the audience for the acquittal of Orestes in *The Eumenides*. She does not, for example, mention the sacrifice of Iphigenia when she attempts to justify the murder of Agamemnon. Much of Clytaemestra's old strength is still apparent. She uses all her wiles to deter Orestes and dies in dignified silence, unlike Agamemnon and Aegisthus.

Orestes' appeal for advice and Pylades' answer have great dramatic effect because Pylades has been silent throughout the play until this point. In his answer Pylades cites the authority of Apollo and gives a kind of divine sanction to the murder of Clytaemestra. Orestes' appeal does not denote any lack of resolution. It reflects a temporary emotional reaction to Clytaemestra in their first meeting since before Agamemnon's death.

FOURTH STASIMON (Lines 934-970)

The chorus sing that they have compassion even for Aegisthus and Clytaemestra. Still, Orestes is alive and Justice, as ever, has triumphed, and these are the best possible developments. The curse on the House of Atreus will be lifted at last. All is well now. The forces of evil have been defeated by Justice and her agent, Time.

EXODOS (Lines 971-1074)

Summary

The doors of the palace open to reveal Orestes standing beside the dead bodies of Aegisthus and Clytaemestra. Servants display the bloodstained netlike robe in which Clytaemestra entangled Agamemnon before she slew him. Pointing to the robe and the corpses, Orestes turns to the chorus and assembled people and justifies his action by citing the crimes committed by his victims and their tyrannous rule over Argos. He has done his duty by avenging Agamemnon, but he admits that it was painful for him to kill his mother, saying, "I have won; but my victory is soiled and has no pride."

As he speaks Orestes becomes restless and agitated. He begins to feel as if he is losing his mind, and insists desperately that the killing of his mother was right and that he acted according to the command of Apollo. But now, he says, he must forfeit the inheritance he has just regained, leave Argos once more, and wander as a homeless outcast.

The chorus try to comfort Orestes by assuring him that his acts were righteous. He barely hears them because he is distracted by the sight of the Furies, grim spirits of vengeance, lying in wait for him. The chorus cannot see anything and think that Orestes' vision is the product of an over-excited imagination, but he cries that the spirits are real and are the avengers threatened in Clytaemestra's dying curse. Orestes loses his last grip on sanity and the madness of guilt comes upon him. He calls to Apollo for help, then runs from the stage with the Furies in hot pursuit.

The chorus sadly watch Orestes go and express the hope that the gods will care for him and that he will find refuge in Apollo's sanctuary at Delphi. They reflect on the ways the curse has manifested itself in three successive generations of the family of Atreus and ask —

> Where
> is the end? Where shall the fury of fate
> be stilled to sleep, be done with?

The chorus exit and the play ends.

Comment

The final scene of *The Choephori* has great dramatic power. In his speech to the people of Argos, Orestes releases all the emotion he has suppressed until now and gives vent to the bitterness he feels. Orestes still believes in the justice of his act and his speech begins on a confident, optimistic note. By the end of the scene, however, he has broken down completely, his mind fails, and he is overwhelmed by a morbid sense of guilt. The intensity of this scene is increased by the dramatic use of the robe in which Clytaemestra trapped Agamemnon. The constant allusions to its netlike quality in the first two plays of the trilogy are a symbolic expression of the way the family of Atreus has been enmeshed in the confusing and inescapable web of fate.

The ending of *The Choephori* has many similarities to the conclusion of *Agamemnon* — Orestes shows the bodies, attempts to justify himself, and begins to break down, just as Clytaemestra showed the bodies, justified herself, and realized despairingly that she would not be able to escape retribution. The reference to Delphi by the chorus foreshadows the outcome of the final play of the trilogy and hints at the ultimate expiation of the curse.

The theme of *The Choephori* is revenge and intrigue. Despite Apollo's intervention, the moral dilemma first presented in *Agamemnon* has not been solved and has resulted in more bloodshed. The chorus, representing humanity, are bewildered by the inability of anyone to challenge or redirect the inexorable hand of fate. It is clear that the old-fashioned morality does not apply to the crimes committed by Clytaemestra and Orestes, for each acted sincerely in support of a legitimate definition of Justice. Somehow, if society is ever to advance to a higher level of civilization, a way must be found to resolve the conflict of these different moral outlooks. The answer Aeschylus puts forward will be found in the final play of the trilogy — *The Eumenides*.

THE EUMENIDES

CHARACTERS

Priestess of Apollo
Apollo
Hermes, the messenger god and patron of travelers (a mute character)
Orestes
Ghost of Clytaemestra
Athene, goddess of wisdom and patroness of the city of Athens.
Chorus of Furies (Eumenides)
Twelve Citizens of Athens, jurors at the trial of Orestes
Athenian Women and Girls, in the final procession

SCENE

Outside the Temple of Apollo at Delphi

TIME

A few days after the closing scene of *The Choephori*

PROLOGUE (Lines 1-63)

Summary

The Priestess of Apollo enters, chanting a prayer to the various divinities that have been associated with the holy shrine of Delphi. Fourth and last in the succession at the sanctuary is Apollo. He has been entrusted with the secrets of prophecy and has been assigned this oracle as the spokesman of his father Zeus.

The priestess goes into the temple. There is a short pause, then she rushes out in terror. She describes the horrible sight she has just seen—a man covered with bloodstains and holding a bloody sword is kneeling at the altar stone in the posture of a suppliant;

asleep on the floor around him are gathered a group of revoltingly ugly creatures dressed in black. The priestess says that this matter is so mysterious that only Apollo himself can unravel it. She exits.

Comment

The recitation of mythological history by the priestess describes the clash between the old and new (Olympian) gods and is the first step in the generalization of Orestes' predicament into a conflict between old and new conceptions of justice.

FIRST EPISODE (Lines 64-142)

Summary

The doors open to reveal the inside of the temple. The scene is as described by the priestess. Apollo and Hermes are standing beside Orestes.

Apollo promises that he will never forsake Orestes. He says that the Furies are creatures from the deepest bowels of the earth, hated as much by the gods as they are by mankind. They will pursue Orestes wherever he goes, but he must endure their torments. Eventually he will arrive at Athens, the holy city of Athene. There he will find sanctuary and his afflictions will come to an end. Apollo absolves Orestes of responsibility for the murder of Clytaemestra by saying, "It was I who made you strike your mother down." He tells Orestes not to lose heart and orders Hermes to watch over him during his wanderings. Apollo goes out, followed by Orestes and Hermes.

Comment

Apollo's acknowledgement of responsibility and prediction that Orestes will be acquitted indicate that the theme of this play is not the personal fate of Orestes. Orestes' trial does not come until later in the play, but its outcome has already been announced and dramatic interest has been shifted to the impending clash between Apollo and the Furies, a conflict between new and old conceptions of justice and different veiws of how to establish and maintain justice on earth.

Summary

A moment later the ghost of Clytaemestra enters. She is en-
raged by the discovery that the Furies have fallen asleep and allowed Orestes, her murderer, to escape. She reviles the chorus for their
failure and reminds them of the many offerings she made to them
while she was still alive. The Furies awaken and angrily realize
that Orestes has eluded them. Clytaemestra urges them to hunt
down the culprit and torment him until his death. She goes out.

Comment

The appearance of Clytaemestra binds this play to *The Choephori* and suggests the full magnitude of Orestes' deed. Her speech
to the Furies underlines their role as enforcers of the ancient law
of blood revenge and opponents of the more progressive moral
attitude represented by Apollo.

FIRST STASIMON (Lines 143-178)

Summary

The Furies awaken and howl angrily about the escape of
Orestes, "the hunted beast." They indignantly claim that Apollo
has stepped beyond the limits of propriety by helping him to get
away. They accuse Apollo and the other "younger gods" of having
gained sovereignty through the use of force, and of lacking respect
for the ancient deities and laws. The Furies shout that Orestes
will never escape them, despite Apollo's interference. The murder
of Clytaemestra eventually will be avenged by a member of the
same family, thus carrying the bloody curse on the family of Atreus
into another generation.

Comment

The weakness of the moral position represented by the Furies
is shown by the prediction in the last lines of this ode that Orestes
will be killed by a member of his own family. The only solution the
Furies can visualize is one in which the law of blood revenge is applied
absolutely, without compassion or understanding. Each succeed-

ing avenger will himself become, like Orestes, a victim of revenge, and the curse will haunt the family forever. The conception of justice held by the Furies is based on strict enforcement of the letter of the law — it has no place for investigation of circumstances, motives, or consequences, no flexibility, and no sense of proportion.

SECOND EPISODE (Lines 179-306)

Summary

Apollo enters again and orders the Furies to leave his temple at once, lest he set loose the power of his sacred arrows against them. He warns that his temple is too holy a place for them to defile by their presence and says that their rightful place is wherever blood is being shed and people are suffering.

The chorus demand that Apollo acknowledge his own guilt in this crime, for it was he who ordered Orestes to commit matricide. Apollo defends himself by saying he ordered Orestes to avenge the murder of Agamemnon. In response the Furies accuse Apollo of having given sanctuary to Orestes despite his bloodguilt, and of having abused them, the divinely ordained avengers of Clytaemestra, in the pursuit of their duty. Apollo points out that the Furies made no effort to punish Clytaemestra for killing Agamemnon. They reply that Agamemnon was not a blood relation of his wife and his murder did not come within their province. Apollo says that marriage is the most sacred of all bonds. If the Furies ignored the murder of a husband by a wife, they have no right to hound Orestes for bringing his father's murderess to justice. The Furies answer defiantly that they will pursue Orestes without mercy and will see him punished for his crime. Apollo says that he will continue to assist the fugitive. The chorus and Apollo exit.

Comment

This is one of the few Greek plays in which there is an exit and re-entrance of the chorus and a complete change of scene. There may also have been a short interval in the production here to allow for the removal and introduction of various pieces of scenery; for example, there is now a statue of Athene on stage that was not present during the first part of the drama.

Summary

The scene changes to Athens, outside the Temple of Athene on the Acropolis. A lapse of several years has taken place. Orestes enters and clings to the feet of Athene's statue as a suppliant. He tells the goddess that he has come in accordance with the advice of Apollo. Long wandering has purged him of his bloodguilt. Now he awaits his trial and her judgment.

PARODOS (Lines 244-275)

The Chorus of Furies re-enter, in hot pursuit of Orestes. They catch sight of him before the statue and gloatingly warn that he cannot escape their wrath by appealing to Athene, for Clytaemestra's death can never be revoked and he must pay for her blood with his own. Hades, the place of dead souls, awaits him.

SECOND EPISODE, continued (Lines 276-306)

Orestes prays to Athene again. He says that it is fitting for him to call upon her now because he has been absolved of his guilt by the cleansing ritual he underwent at the Temple of Apollo shortly after the murder, and by his long years of wandering and suffering. Orestes tells Athene that if she saves him and sets him free at last, he and the kingdom of Aegos will be the perpetual allies of Athens.

SECOND STASIMON (Lines 307-395)

Summary

The chorus state that their eternal function is to punish criminals and avenge unpunished murders. They do not harm the innocent, but when a man is stained with guilt, as Orestes is, they haunt him until his evil deeds have been paid for in full. They call on the spirit of Night, their mother, to witness Apollo's efforts to hinder them in the pursuit of their duties. They say that their function was given to them at the very dawn of time and they are implacable in carrying it out. They are feared by all men. Even the gods cannot interfere with the Furies, for their role was assigned them by Destiny.

Comment

The ancient conception of justice represented by the Furies is explained in this ode. They stand for the primitive *lex talionis*, or law of retaliation — the criminal is punished by being made the victim of the same crime he committed ("an eye for an eye"), the ties of blood kinship are the most sacred of human bonds. These ideas are the legal basis for the bloodfeuds that were common in ancient Greece and for the tragic experiences of the family of Atreus recounted in this trilogy.

Certain stanzas of this ode are known to scholars as the "binding-song" or "binding-spell," because the words have an almost hypnotic quality in Greek and seem intended as an effort to entrance and trap Orestes by magical means.

THIRD EPISODE (Lines 396-489)

Summary

Athene enters, having heard Orestes' prayer in far-off Troy, where she was taking possession of land allotted to Athens by the victorious Greek chieftains. She is not frightened by the Furies, despite their horrible appearance, and asks them and the stranger kneeling before her statue to explain their presence outside her temple. She reminds them all that her sacred precinct is a place of justice.

The Furies explain that Orestes is guilty of matricide. After questioning them further, Athene remarks that they seem more concerned with the forms of justice than with justice itself. The Furies invite her to interrogate Orestes and decide for herself about his guilt. Athene agrees, but insists that the final authority of judgment in the case be given to her. The chorus confidently accepts her proposal.

Athene turns to Orestes and asks for his side of the story. He states again that he is no suppliant because he has already been purified for his crime. Orestes identifies himself to Athene, tells how Agamemnon was treacherously murdered by Clytaemestra on his return home from Troy, and how he later came back from exile and killed his mother to avenge his father's death. He says that Apollo shares the responsibility for his crime because the god ordered him to commit matricide and threatened terrible retribution if he failed to obey. "This is my case," Orestes says, "Decide if it be right or wrong./ I am in your hands. Where my fate falls, I shall accept."

Athene reflects for a moment, then states that this is a matter too complex for any single mortal to judge and that even she does not have the right to decide the issue alone. It is a serious legal and moral dilemma, but since she has taken the case on herself, she will establish a special court made up of the finest of her citizens to hear the evidence and come to a decision. Athene goes out to select the jurors, promising that, "They shall swear to make no judgment that is not just, and make clear where in this action the truth lies."

Comment

Athene's attitude in this scene implies that the trial will be concerned with things of far greater importance than the merely technical question of whether or not Orestes is guilty of matricide. Her refusal to arbitrate the case herself and the establishment of a special new court represent the replacement of archaic, autocratic justice with the new form of civic justice, in which an entire society unites to determine and enforce its conceptions of right and wrong.

THIRD STASIMON (Lines 490-565)

Summary

The chorus warn of the danger of leniency toward crime. If Orestes is acquitted, all the old laws will be overthrown. Justice will come to an end and evil will become dominant. Men will commit crimes without fear of punishment.

Fear of authority and punishment is an essential element of society, the foundation of all law and order, for it restrains men from crime. It is themselves, the Furies, who embody this authority. They never harm good men who are innocent of evil, but hunt down and punish all transgressors.

Man should seek neither the license of anarchy nor the slavery of tyranny, but the middle path, where freedom and law are judiciously balanced, and where good behavior that proceeds from goodness of heart is rewarded. Above all, the chorus say, there must be reverence for justice, for sin begets sin and the evil always perish.

Comment

This choral ode continues the generalization of the case, to the point where it is predicted that the acquittal of Orestes will result in the demoralization of society and the complete breakdown of law and order. There is much to recommend the Furies' point that authority is one of the foundations of civilization, as will be acknowledged by Athene before the conclusion of the play.

FOURTH EPISODE (Lines 566-766)

Summary

Athene enters, followed by the twelve jurors and a herald. Other citizens of Athens assemble to observe the trial. Apollo comes in with Orestes and announces that he intends to assist the defendant. Athene calls the new court to order and invites the Furies, as plaintiffs, to begin the trial by presenting their case.

The chorus question Orestes. He admits having killed Clytaemestra, but says that he was ordered to commit the crime by Apollo. He demands to know why the Furies did not punish Clytaemestra for the murder of Agamemnon. They reply that Clytaemestra has already been punished by her death at his hands. Besides, since Agamemnon was not her blood relation, his murder has no bearing on this case. Confused by the course his trial is taking, Orestes asks Apollo to speak for him. Orestes says that he willingly admits the murder, but does not himself know whether he did right or wrong.

Apollo asserts that all the oracles he has ever spoken, whether pertaining to man, woman, or city, have been in accordance with the will of Zeus. The oracle by which he commanded Orestes to murder his mother was no exception and embodied the express wishes of Zeus. And, he warns the jurors, the will of Zeus has more force than the oaths they have taken to judge according to their own understanding of the case.

So in other words, the chorus remark, Zeus himself said that Orestes could murder his mother with impunity. Apollo ignores this and says that the death of Agamemnon is not to be compared with that of Clytaemestra, for Agamemnon was a great man and a king, and was killed by treachery ill-suited to his station in life.

The chorus reply that Apollo seems to be suggesting that Zeus regards the murder of a father as the most serious of crimes, yet Zeus himself bound his own father Cronos in chains. How can he reconcile these contradictions? This question makes Apollo violently angry and he insults the Furies as "foul animals." He says that Zeus can undo the chains that bind Cronos and make good the harm that was done, but murder is final and can never be undone.

The chorus ask whether Apollo has considered how one who has shed his mother's blood, an act of absolute finality for which there is no atonement, can ever again return to his homeland or participate in religious rituals.

Apollo answers that the mother is not a blood relation of the child, but only the nurse of the seed planted in her by the true parent, the father. Thus Orestes has incurred no bloodguilt. As proof of this doctrine Apollo cites Athene herself, for legend said that she was born full-grown from the forehead of her father, Zeus. Apollo concludes his speech by promising greatly to increase the wealth and power of Athens if Orestes is acquitted.

Athene turns the case over to the jurors for their decision and formally establishes this new tribunal—the Court of the Areopagus —to endure forever and to have jurisdiction in all cases of manslaughter. She advises the jurymen to judge and govern in justice and not to drive out fear from their city, for the man who fears nothing cannot be righteous. This court, she says, will be a shrine of justice, the greatest strength of her holy city. Nothing will corrupt it. As "a sentry on the land," it will forever protect the innocent and punish the guilty. She urges the jurors to meditate on the meaning of their oaths and arrive at a decision.

The Furies and Apollo threaten the jurors with reprisals if they lose the case, then begin to bicker with each other. Meanwhile, Athene announces that in the event of a tie she will cast her vote in favor of Orestes. She says this is because she had no mother and thus must support the rights of the father, and also because she likes men, although not enough to marry one.

The jurors cast their votes. There are six for conviction, six for acquittal. Athene votes for acquittal also and Orestes is declared a free man. The former defendant joyfully thanks Athene and solemnly vows that for all time the people of Argos, his homeland, will be the friends and allies of the Athenians. He wishes the best of success and fortune to Athens, then leaves with Apollo.

Comment

Since one purpose of this scene is to give the prestige of divine sanction to the legal processes in Athens, this trial has many similarities to the way in which trials were actually conducted in the time of Aeschylus. Among these similarities are the preliminary hearing to determine jurisdiction, the privilege of the accused to speak last, the rule that the accused be acquitted if the votes of the jurors are equal, the repeated exhortations to the jurors to remember their oaths, and the right of the plaintiff to prosecute his own case. The ancient homicide court of the Areopagus was one of the most revered legal institutions in fifth century Athens. The interesting account of its origin given by Aeschylus must have made his complex story seem particularly pertinent in the eyes of his audience.

Apollo acts as the advocate of Orestes at the trial, but the defense he presents is far from adequate. This is because the Furies, despite their primitive nature, protect sacred bonds of kinship and blood that cannot be ignored. Although he is a god, Apollo cannot negate their position because it is an essential constituent of an ordered society. His arguments for Orestes have been made weak to emphasize that neither side in this dispute is entirely right.

In his first speech Apollo tries to influence the jurors by an appeal to authority rather than to reason. By including oracles pertaining to cities in his claim always to have expressed the will of Zeus, Apollo puts his political and moral oracles on a par. The Delphic oracle was notorious for having made some serious mistakes in political matters, most particularly when it opposed resistance to the Persian invasion. The jurors are bound to wonder whether Apollo's morality may not be as subject to error as his politics.

In his second speech Apollo attacks Clytaemestra for killing Agamemnon by treachery, but Orestes killed Clytaemestra by treachery also, and did so in accordance with Apollo's own command. In addition, Apollo implies that there is no difference between matricide and any other form of murder, a view that would probably offend the jurors. While describing Agamemnon's greatness in life, Apollo inadvertently alludes to the sacrifice of Iphigenia, an incident bound to increase sympathy for Clytaemestra at a moment when he is trying to emphasize her wickedness.

Apollo's third speech is weak because the murder of a woman is as final as that of a man. The theory of parenthood presented in Apollo's final speech is farfetched and denies the intimate emotional bond between mothers and their sons, another point that might offend the jurors. Finally, Apollo concludes with a shameless offer to bribe the jurors if they vote in favor of Orestes.

The case presented by Apollo is so unsatisfactory that it would appear Aeschylus used the framework of a debate as the basis for a dramatic confrontation between adversaries, and made no real effort at a well-reasoned analysis of the particular case under discussion. The reason for this is made clear when the jurors vote. They are tied because the case is too hard for human beings to judge. There is justice on both sides—neither the ties of kinship nor the requirements of authority and the social order can be denied. Athene casts the deciding vote as the first step in the establishment of a new and greater social and moral order, in which the desirable elements of the views represented by the Furies and the Olympian gods are combined. It is interesting to note that Athene's reason for voting to acquit Orestes is morally irrelevant to the issue on trial, a final reminder that there can be no arbitrary solutions to moral problems.

The trial of Orestes is important in dramatic history because it is the first extended scene in which three speaking actors and the chorus (here actually used as a fourth speaking actor) all take important parts in the action at once. There is a difficult transition at the end of the scene where Orestes and Apollo drop out of the action before the conclusion of the play, but Aeschylus handles this effectively by giving emphasis to the dissatisfaction and threats of the chorus and letting these carry over into the next *episode*.

FOURTH STASIMON (Lines 777-792)

The chorus say that the younger gods are destroying all the ancient laws and that they have been dishonored and disinherited by the decision of the court. They swear to avenge themselves by setting loose all their evil powers on the land of Athens.

FIFTH EPISODE and EXODOS (Lines 793-1047)

Summary

Athene tries to conciliate the Furies by pointing out that they were not defeated or disgraced by the court's decision. Since the vote was a tie and the voice of Zeus himself was heard at the trial, speaking through his oracle Apollo, she says, justice has indeed prevailed. She urges the Furies to subdue their anger against Athens and promises to give them a sanctuary of their own in the city, where the citizens can worship them and make offerings.

The chorus repeat their threats and insist that they have been insulted by the Athenians. Athene pleads with them to reconsider. She tells them to be reasonable, to accept the will of Zeus and the honors offered them by Athens.

The Furies lament the unjust treatment they have received. They say their ancient rights have been taken away. Athene replies that she will tolerate their anger because they are older and wiser than she is. Still, she has wisdom also, and her advice to accept the loving offer of a home in Athens is wise. She says, "Do good. Receive good, and be honored as the good/ are honored. Share our country, the beloved of god."

Athene repeats this offer and promises even more benefits until the Furies begin to calm down. Her offer has aroused their interest. They begin to listen carefully and ask eager questions. There is great attraction to them in her promise of a place of perpetual honor and utility in Athens. Finally they accept. They begin to pronounce blessings on the land instead of the curses they had threatened earlier.

Athene and the Furies join together in a responsive lyrical description of the brilliant future that awaits Athens, now that "holy persuasion" has replaced violence. The Furies are renamed the Eumenides, or "kindly ones," in recognition of their new character, for they are now benevolent spirits instead of personifications of vengeance and misfortune.

Meanwhile, the women and girls of Athens have assembled with lighted torches to welcome the Eumenides. They form up together in ranks and escort the chorus from the stage in a great parade that is meant to represent the Pan-Athenaic Procession. As they march out, all the participants join together in a hymn which concludes —

> There shall be peace forever between these people
> of Pallas [Athene] and their guests. Zeus the all
> seeing
> met with Destiny to confirm it.
> Singing all follow our footsteps.

The play ends.

Comment

The Eumenides end on an exalted note of reconciliation and optimism. Orestes and his family have no part in the closing scene of the play. Their absence at the moment of resolution, and the knowledge that the trial of Orestes was conducted on extraneous grounds and really solved nothing, indicate that their role in the trilogy is symbolic. Aeschylus used the story of the family of Atreus to provide illustrative material for his analysis of the central issue of the trilogy—the nature of justice.

At the conclusion of the trilogy the Furies, who were originally the uncompromising agents of destiny and divine retribution, are mystically converted into benevolent spirits, although their insistence that authority and discipline are essential components of society is heeded. A new social and moral dispensation is established by Zeus, through his daughter Athene, the personification of wisdom. Justice will now be secured by an impartial and rational human court. The new justice will be tempered by mercy and understanding, as in the trial of Orestes. The sacred institutions of Athens are glorified as the pattern of earthly justice and happiness. "Holy persuasion," reason, is the civilizing instrument of the new order.

The closing pageant binds together all elements of the new harmony—primitive and modern, divine and human—and the brilliant pageant, an imitation of Athens' most holy festival, symbolizes the fulfillment of man's long and painful groping toward a satisfactory organization of society. Mankind at last is liberated from the prison of ignorance, fear, and hatred.

THE CHARACTERS

CLYTAEMESTRA

Clytaemestra is the only character to appear in all three plays of the trilogy. She dominates the action of Agamemnon, but has smaller roles in the other two plays. Many critics consider Clytaemestra the most impressive and fascinating woman in Greek tragedy. Her most important characteristic, as pointed out by the watchman in *Agamemnon* is her "male strength of heart." She is proud, efficient, shrewd, and strong, and all these traits come into play when, practically unaided and without arousing suspicion, she plans and carries out a plot to commit murder. Indeed, Clytaemestra is so confident and so superior to those around her, including Agamemnon, that she often alludes to her plans more or less openly without fear of being detected. Clytaemestra is by far the strongest character in the play. This is most clearly demonstrated when, at various points, she forces Agamemnon, Aegisthus, and the Elders of Argos to bend to her will.

Although the trilogy covers a period of several years, Aeschylus does not show any changes in Clytaemestra's personality. This may be because any sign of weakness or remorse on her part would have lessened sympathy for Orestes in the last two plays, but it should also be remembered that Aeschylus' main interest as a tragedian was to dramatize conflicts between opposing forces or individuals, and not to examine the inner development of particular characters.

ORESTES

Orestes is the central figure of the trilogy. He is the main character of the second and third plays, and, though he does not appear in *Agamemnon,* he is mentioned frequently and his return home is predicted.

Orestes' most important characteristic is his belief in the justice of his cause and his determination to carry out the command of Apollo despite the moral and emotional qualms he occasionally feels. After the slaying of Clytaemestra, Orestes is embittered and on the verge of madness, but he never doubts that he has done the right thing. Even years of torment by the Furies in *The Eumenides* do not weaken this belief. Thus, though his dilemma is real and frightening, Orestes is a one-dimensional character who cannot arouse real empathy. That Aeschylus intended this is shown in *The Eumenides,* where Orestes is turned into a human symbol in the great moral conflict that is fought out on stage between

Apollo, as representative of Zeus, and the Furies, as representative of the primitive, pre-Olympian religion. Orestes drops out of the action before the final scene of the play. He is completely forgotten while the conflict is resolved by Athene and the remaining segment of the play concentrates on glorification of the Athenian way of life.

ELECTRA

Electra does not have anything near the importance given her by Sophocles and Euripides in their plays based on the same legend. Aeschylus uses her mainly to provide information for Orestes and to help strengthen his resolution by her presence. She has no real part in the plot to kill Clytaemestra and Aegisthus, and disappears early in *The Choephori,* the only play of the trilogy in which she appears.

AGAMEMNON

Agamemnon is a powerful king, a great conqueror and leader of men, but as characterized by Aeschylus he has certain crucial weaknesses that lead to his downfall. Agamemnon is complacent, egotistical, and shallow. In his dramatic confrontation with Clytaemestra, Agamemnon blusters a bit and echoes some conventional religious sentiments, but he is easily trapped by her wily use of his own defects as weapons against him. Clytaemestra murders Agamemnon to avenge Iphigenia, but would not have succeeded if his other sins — the desecration of the Trojan temples and his sacrilegious insolence in walking on the tapestry — had not aroused the wrath of the gods against him.

AEGISTHUS

Aegisthus appears briefly in *Agamemnon* and *The Choephori.* Through an old enemy of Agamemnon and an accomplice in his murder, Aegisthus seems at base to be an ordinary man with no special attributes. He has common sense and some political ability, but is no match for Clytaemestra, the woman whom he aids and eventually marries. In *The Choephori* it is clear that Clytaemestra is the real ruler of Argos, though she pays Aegisthus some deference for the sake of appearances, since he is a man and therefore officially the king.

OTHER CHARACTERS

Apollo — god of the sun and prophecy. He appears as the defender of Orestes in *The Eumenides*.

Athene — goddess of wisdom and patroness of Athens. In *The Eumenides* she establishes the new court, casts the deciding vote at the trial of Orestes, and afterward placates the Furies.

Cassandra — the prophetess daughter of the king of Troy, she is the concubine of Agamemnon in *Agamemnon*.

Cilissa — the former nurse of Orestes in *The Choephori*.

A Herald — announces the return of the army in *Agamemnon*.

Hermes — the messenger god and patron of travelers, a mute character in *The Eumenides*.

A Priestess — at the temple of Apollo in Delphi, she speaks the prologue of *The Eumenides*.

Pylades — the companion of Orestes in *The Choephori*.

A Watchman — speaks the prologue of *Agamemnon*.

CHORUSES

The Elders of Argos, in *Agamemnon*.

Captive Serving Women, in *The Choephori*.

The Furies, in *The Eumenides*.

SUGGESTED READING

Graves, Robert. *The Greek Myths.* Baltimore, 1955 (paperback).

Hadas, Moses. *A History of Greek Literature.* New York, 1962 (paperback).

Harsh, Philip W. *A Handbook of Classical Drama.* Stanford, Calif., 1944.

Kitto, H. D. F. *Greek Tragedy: A Literary Study.* Garden City, N.Y., 1950 (paperback).

Lucas, D. W. *The Greek Tragic Poets.* New York, 1959 (paperback).

Murray, Gilbert. *Aeschylus: The Creator of Tragedy.* Oxford, 1940.

Norwood, Gilbert. *Greek Tragedy.* New York, 1960 (paperback).

Sheppard, J. T. *Aeschylus and Sophocles: Their Work and Influence.* New York, 1927.

EXAMINATION QUESTIONS

1. Give a brief account of the legendary background of *The Oresteia.* Mention some tragedies based on elements of this legend by Greek dramatists other than Aeschylus.

2. Who speaks the prologue to *Agamemnon?* What is the purpose of this speech?

3. How is Agamemnon ultimately responsible for his own downfall? What sins is he guilty of committing?

4. How are Aeschylus' religious doctrines that wisdom is learned through suffering and that retribution comes to all sinners illustrated in *Agamemnon?* What attitude about Zeus and the Olympian gods is implied in *Agamemnon?*

5. Discuss the characterization of Clytaemestra in *Agamemnon.* What sort of woman is she? Why does she plot to murder her husband? Why is there little exploration of her emotional and psychological state?

6. What attitude about the Trojan War is stated in the odes of the chorus and the speech of the herald in *Agamemnon?* How does

Aeschylus symbolically relate the fall of Troy to the fate of Agamemnon?

7. What is the purpose of the herald's account of the fate of Menelaus?

8. At what point does the dramatic climax of *Agamemnon* take place? Discuss the confrontation of Agamemnon and Clytaemestra. What does she want him to do and why? What is his initial reaction? How does she force him to give in to her wishes?

9. What story about herself is told by Cassandra? Why does the chorus ignore her prophecies? How does her speech broaden the meaning of the entire trilogy?

10. How does Clytaemestra behave after the murder of Agamemnon? What role does Aegisthus play in the final scene of *Agamemnon?*

11. Why does Orestes return to Argos? How much time has passed since the events in *Agamemnon?* Why does Orestes hide when Electra approaches?

12. How does Orestes identify himself to Electra? What signs that he was back had she already discovered? What is the purpose of this recognition scene? In what other Greek tragedy is this scene parodied?

13. Why is the portrayal of Orestes' personality one-dimensional? What is his dominant characteristic? What is the moral dilemma he faces? How is the oracle of Apollo responsible for his predicament?

14. How does Aeschylus' portrayal of Electra differ from those of Sophocles and Euripides? What is her role in *The Choephori?*

15. What is the meaning of the long lyrical passage at the tomb of Agamemnon in *The Choephori?* Who are the participants? What are their motives?

16. Give an account of Clytaemestra's dream, its meaning and poetic use.

17. Who is Cilissa? What is her role in *The Choephori?*

18. How does the chorus take an active part in the plot to kill Aegisthus and Clytaemestra? What is the effect of its interference?

19. How does Aegisthus react to the news that Orestes is dead? What is the relationship of Aegisthus to Clytaemestra?

20. Why does Orestes hesitate and turn to Pylades for advice before killing Clytaemestra? What does Pylades tell him? Why does this answer have great dramatic effect?

21. How does Clytaemestra behave when facing death? Does her character seem to have changed in the time since the events in *Agamemnon?*

22. How does Orestes react after killing his mother? What similarities are there between the endings of *Agamemnon* and *The Choephori?* What is the moral dilemma at the close of *The Choephori?*

23. Who speaks the prologue to *The Eumenides?* How does this speech generalize Orestes' predicament into a conflict between old and new conceptions of justice?

24. How is dramatic interest shifted away from the fate of Orestes in the conversation between Orestes and Apollo in the first scene of *The Eumenides?* What conflict is made the central theme of the play?

25. What purpose is served by the appearance of Clytaemestra's ghost?

26. What are the Furies? What moral principles do they enforce? Why is it that they never attempted to punish Clytaemestra for the murder of Agamemnon? Is the concept of *lex talionis* also found in the Bible?

27. What are the two conceptions of justice that are opposed at the trial of Orestes? By whom are they represented? Why does Athene establish a new court for the trial? Why is Orestes eventually acquitted on grounds that are irrelevant to the case?

28. How does Athene placate the Furies after the acquittal of Orestes? What is the meaning of their new name? What moral

principles upheld by them will be maintained in the new social order?

29. Why does Orestes drop out of the action before the final scene of *The Eumenides?* What symbolic use has Aeschylus made of the story of the family of Atreus?

30. How is the conflict in *The Eumenides* resolved? What are the elements of the new social and moral dispensation and what is its guiding principle? What is the purpose of the glorification of the Athenian way of life at the end of the play? What is the meaning of the closing pageant?

31. Discuss the main philosophical and religious themes of *The Oresteia.* What is the place of *The Oresteia* in the history of drama?

32. Discuss Aristotle's definitions of tragedy and the tragic hero and their application to the three plays of *The Oresteia.*

33. Give a brief account of Aeschylus' career as a tragedian, mentioning the innovations for which he is responsible and some of his more important dramatic works.

34. Identify by play and function the following characters: Cassandra, Aegisthus, Pylades, Electra, Athene, Cilissa, Apollo, Hermes, A Priestess, A Watchman, A Herald.

35. Identify the following figures in the legend that provides the background of *The Oresteia:* Iphigenia, Helen, Menelaus, Paris, Thyestes, Atreus, Calchas, Artemis.

36. Define: prologue, parodos, episode, stasimon, exodos, orchestra, skene, thymele, Thespis, dithyramb, *Poetics, Proteus,* trilogy, tetralogy, City Dionysia, Theater of Dionysus, Trojan War, Argos, Phocis, Sparta, Aulis, Delphi, Court of the Areopagus.